Din Learning Design Almanac

A little book of big ideas

ding.global

Published by Ding Learning Publishing
First published in Great Britain 2024

Printed and bound in Great Britain by Short Run Press Ltd

978-1-7385009-0-1

ding.global

Illustrations by Emily Clarkson

We cannot teach another person directly; we can only facilitate their learning.

Carl Rogers

Ding is a **creative learning design agency.**

Their mission is to transform lives through awesome learning design. They build courses and programmes, train learning designers, and tackle complex problems using learning design tools and techniques.

If you're wondering what learning design is, don't worry - it isn't obvious. Here are some suggestions that might help:

- **Learning design is the act of making deliberate decisions about the many factors that influence learning.**
- **It involves defining what needs to be learned, then identifying the most pragmatic ways of enabling someone to learn it.**
- **It's about finding the most appropriate mix of technologies and activities for a particular learning experience.**
- **It helps businesses develop training programmes that equip employees with the knowledge and skills to deliver the strategy.**
- **It enables universities and training providers to design courses that maximise the chances of learners succeeding.**
- **Above all, it's about making learning effective, enjoyable, transformative and memorable.**

The Ding team have worked with established businesses, startups, universities, colleges and individuals to design and deliver transformative learning experiences. They run sprints, bootcamps and workshops to help people use learning design in their own professional context.

You can read their case studies, watch their videos, listen to their podcasts and say hello at **ding.global**

Why write a book about learning design? What is learning design anyway? Who needs it? And where is it useful?

Over the last few years, the Ding team have asked ourselves these questions repeatedly. We're a small team of educators who care deeply about learning, and about how effective teaching can transform people's lives. This book represents our attempts to make sense of learning design, and why it matters.

Ding is a learning design agency on a mission to create exceptional learning experiences. We launched Ding in April 2020, just as the global pandemic was starting. In the months that followed, we interviewed people, ran workshops and courses, hosted online events and generally did everything we could to help people adapt their courses for online delivery.

Like many others, we learned a lot about learning design in a short time. So, we thought we'd pull together the highlights in Ding's Learning Design Almanac. Creating the book provided an opportunity for us to reflect on the conversations, podcasts, workshops and projects that have revealed a wealth of tips, tricks and techniques for producing effective learning experiences.

You can read it end-to-end or dip in and out. We've designed it to be bite-sized, so whatever page you turn to you'll find something useful.

We hope you enjoy it as much as we enjoyed putting it together!

Tony Reeves

Phil Gomm

Ray Martin

Nicholas Houghton

ding

Tony's Story

The first time I realised I was interested in learning was shortly after I started teaching in a university. I was running a seminar with a class of music students, and at the end of the seminar I asked them to share their key takeaways on a discussion board. A few days later, I was perplexed as to why none of them had done what I asked.

This experience was the start of a very long journey in which I became fascinated by the role of digital technologies in learning. I got a job as a 'learning technologist' and had the opportunity to work with lots of creative educators, helping them use digital technologies effectively with their own students. One of these was the amazing Phil Gomm, the person with whom I would eventually co-found Ding.

I became a student on the university's teacher training course. Thanks to the guidance of the inspirational course leader, Dr. Gill Nah, I obtained another key piece of the puzzle I was trying to solve – learning theories. While many people found theories boring, to me they were incredibly useful ways of understanding the different ways in which learning happens. This led me to embark on a PhD in education, focusing on the role of digital technologies in learning.

It was during this time that I stumbled across the theory of critical pedagogy. Of all the theories I'd encountered so far, this one really blew my mind. It completely changed my view of what teaching was – and what it could be.

Soon afterwards, I was fortunate to be offered the chance to lead a teacher training course. This gave me the opportunity to work closely with Dr Nicholas Houghton and Ray Martin, and learn from their extensive knowledge of curriculum design, assessment and inclusivity. This was the next piece of the learning puzzle.

And then suddenly... there was a pandemic.

While up to that point, many educators had seen online learning as a 'nice to have', it was now essential to be able to teach effectively online. Suddenly, the need to know how to design and deliver effective learning experiences was top of the educational agenda. This planted the seed that there might be an opportunity to reach and support more people than was possible through the teacher training course.

And so, after much consideration, I jumped. There's an old Zen saying: 'leap and the net will appear'. And fortunately, it did. I called up Phil, and together we founded the Ding learning design agency. Phil is one of the most inspirational and creative educators I've ever met, and by combining our skills I realised we could take on a whole range of learning design work.

Phil is also a film buff, and it was when he suggested I watch several films by director Wes Anderson that the concept of Ding really started to take shape. His films are quirky, fun, and beautifully designed. And I felt there was a need for more of this in learning design and educational development.

And so here we are. Ding's mission is to help people create beautifully designed and transformative learning experiences. Our aim is to provide practical, accessible advice to guide learning design. We're learning design nerds, and we care about each and every factor that can influence the effectiveness of a learning experience.

I'm incredibly grateful to all the people I've met on our journey so far. They have helped us figure out what learning design actually *is*, and where it can add value (which, it turns out, is in more places than you might expect). The conversations with our clients, colleagues and the wider learning design community have all shown us why the world needs better learning design.

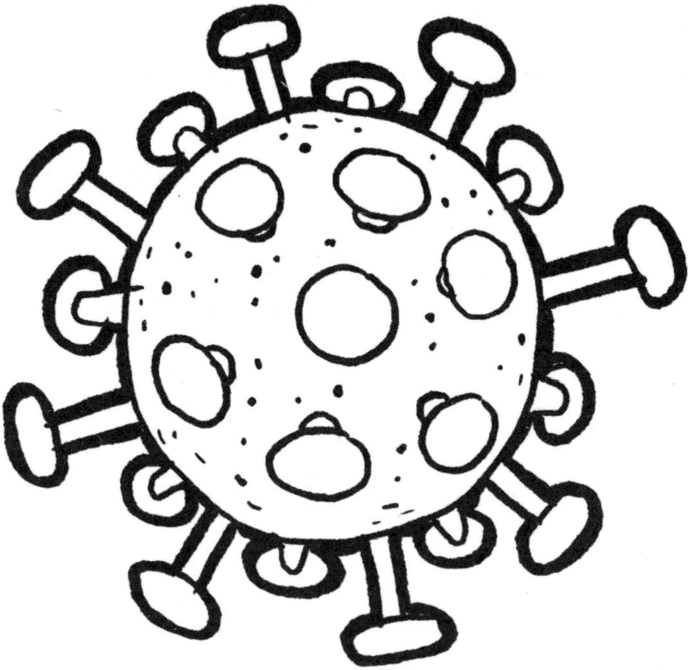

Ding's Covid Diaries

Ding was founded in the midst of the COVID-19 pandemic, a disruption to the status quo that prompted all of us to reassess our practices and values.

Amid this global challenge, we engaged educators in candid conversations about their experiences in adapting and transforming to 'the new normal'. Simultaneously, our team pondered their own responses to these extraordinary circumstances.

Ding's COVID Diaries capture just some of these reflections, as we consider what the pandemic taught us about effective learning design.

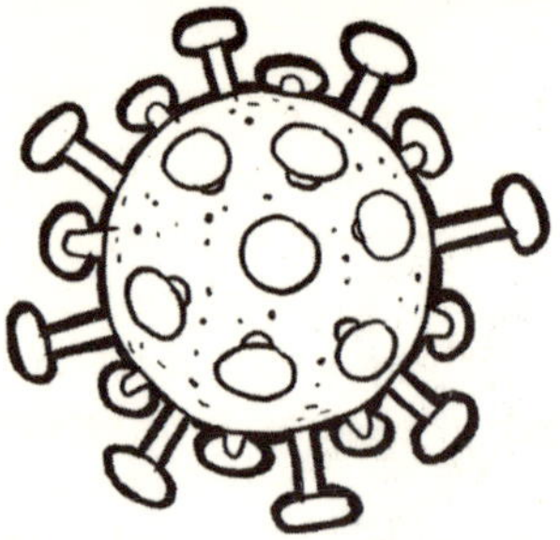

Ding's Covid Diaries: Meghana Bisineer Part 1, August 2020

Insights from a year of teaching remotely

I've been teaching at California College of the Arts for four years now. I'm on a tenure track, and in your third year, you get to go on a sabbatical, which is really amazing. It's a one-semester break where you can focus entirely on your own work. So, it was a lot of preparation to get to the point where I could say, "I'm free, and I'm going." I wasn't going to be here for a whole semester, and I was really hungry for that dedicated studio time.

I had plans for a residency in Mexico, a fellowship in Italy, and a visit to my parents in India. I was looking forward to spending time there and also seeing what I could create. Then, I would head back to California to work in my studio and prepare for the semester. However, when I went online to buy my ticket for Italy, I noticed there were three cases of COVID nearby...

I contacted them, and they reassured me everything was going ahead. I didn't want to cancel, but as time went on, things became more uncertain. I decided to come to London, where I have a British passport. The California College of the Arts declared we would be completely online for the fall semester. So, now I'm fully focused on preparing for online classes.

Before COVID, online teaching wasn't the norm. It was very much about being in the classroom, having face-to-face interactions, and being present in workshops. Now, we're navigating a shift to this new way of working. The challenge lies in recreating the sense of community and support in a virtual setting.

Teaching animation isn't just about imparting technical skills; it's about fostering a way of thinking. It's about encouraging students to question, create, and tell their own stories. In a virtual setting, paying attention to student engagement and feedback becomes a challenge. I used to rely on in-person cues, and adapting to a virtual classroom requires a different approach.

So, while the shift to online teaching presents its challenges, it also opens up opportunities to explore new ways of learning and connecting with students. It's about finding the right balance and using the available tools to create a meaningful and engaging learning experience.

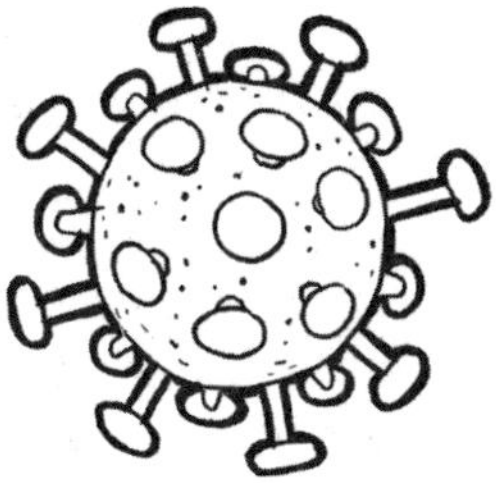

Tears for fears: on the bereavement of teachers

Phil Gomm, February 2021

These past strange months, I've talked with, Zoomed with, and mentored, a large number of teachers meeting the changes wrought by Covid with varying levels of enthusiasm and confidence. In some ways, I find myself in the role of the 'smiling face' of change management, as I work with tutors to help them feel more at home in the online teaching space - even going as far as suggesting how some of the characteristics of online learning might *enhance* their teaching more generally, which I believe. A large part of the successes of my tenure as course leader stemmed from my early embrace of online communities in support of learning and student engagement, and from 'flipping the classroom' through making available a rich curricula of quality online video resources.

More recently, I talked with a senior lecturer, who admitted to feeling physically nauseous at the thought of *another* day in front of his laptop; another day, on his own, in his room, his face pushed up against the faces of his students, yet devoid also of contact with them, and likewise his colleagues, and without all the smaller, less tangible things once combining to produce the culture of his course and its successes. Green around the gills and exhausted, he watches all of this from his strange remove, as all the things that once felt certain struggle to remain so, his own identity included.

This is the special hopelessness of the bereaved, the secret they keep for fear of appearing weak or uncooperative. Despite the acuity of their loss, despite their discombobulation, they still get up, get dressed, feed themselves, feed the cat - and teach on Microsoft Teams to a classroom of learners with their cameras off.

I'm seeing bereavement everywhere. Sure, individuals are grieving the way things 'used to be', but not, I think, because they're Luddites, or dinosaurs deserving of a jolly big meteor, but rather because their identities are in crisis. They are not who they used to be, and yet the speed of change in the sector insists they bury these feelings in order to satisfy everyone else. Worse, there is as much shame around as you want: shame, because you don't know how to use Zoom or Teams or Classroom or whatever; shame, because a part of you cannot be bothered to grow, or learn, or adapt, while your heart still smarts; shame, because you suspect your students are unhappy (which they likely are, because, yes, they're grieving too); and shame, because you just want things to go back the way they were while other bright and shiny people proselytise about the future; and where there's shame, there's resentment, and where there is resentment, there is anger, and so it goes.

So, I never think, 'Oh no! Here is *another* late-adopter'. I don't think, 'Why are some academics so bloody difficult?' I'm thinking, here is just another someone estranged from who they once where and what they once knew how to do, and I'm minded to read frustration, reluctance, resistance and 'shut-downness' for what it likely is; bereavement working its way out.

There's a reason the sympathy cards we buy don't say *'This Isn't A Loss! It's An Opportunity!'*

There's a reason change takes time.

"A big part of being a learning designer is ensuring that the person delivering the session feels confident. Phil's analogy of bereavement really captures the sense of loss that many educators felt in the shift to teaching online.

The pandemic taught us that resistance to online delivery wasn't merely a refusal to adapt, it was a sign that educators were in mourning. Not only had they lost the familiarity of the physical classroom, they had also lost part of their identity as a teacher and felt vulnerable as a result.

Phil's article is a poignant reminder that learning designers need to tread carefully when discussing different modes of delivery. Teaching and facilitating is a performance, and if the person delivering an experience feels vulnerable they won't perform well."

Ding's Hot Takeaways!

At Ding, we're passionate about translating our insights, conversations, reflections, and professional experiences into straightforward, practical advice for learning designers.

Look out for our Ding's Hot Takeaways, useful and easy-to-apply hints and tips for feeding-up your learning design. Yum.

Ding's Hot Takeaway: Managing Change

Learning designers should approach educators with empathy, acknowledge their emotions, and provide the necessary support and resources for a successful transition to new teaching methods or technologies. Balancing sensitivity with the promotion of growth and adaptation is crucial in the process. Consider these eight takeaways:

1. **Empathise and Acknowledge Feelings:** Recognise and address educators' emotional responses to change.
2. **Respect The Pace:** Allow educators to embrace new methods at their own speed.
3. **Integrate Technology Thoughtfully:** Blend technology with teaching principles for an enhanced learning experience.
4. **Encourage Continuous Growth:** Foster a mindset of ongoing learning and development.
5. **Provide Emotional Support:** Prioritise the well-being of educators and offer resources for mental health.
6. **Establish Open Communication:** Create an environment where educators can freely express concerns and seek assistance.
7. **Offer Diverse Learning Support:** Cater to varied learning styles with options like workshops, tutorials, and peer support.
8. **Advocate for Quality Online Learning:** Stress the importance of effective strategies for maintaining high-quality education in online settings.

Phil's Story

In truth, I don't go to many dinner parties, but when I do, and people ask me about my job, to which I reply, 'learning design,' they tend to look at me rather blankly. They quickly confuse 'learning designer' with being a teacher or working in a specific school or university, and shortly after that, they're inclined to glaze over. Let's face it; defining learning design is tricky, because it all gets a bit *meta*. Learning design is a discipline about the art, craft and graft of explaining other disciplines. So, there I am, explaining the explaining of explaining... Little wonder I don't get invited to many dinner parties.

Sometimes we might get as far as a second question. Sometimes I get asked, '*Why* are you a learning designer?' and I always find this question much easier to answer and I do it by sharing two anecdotes, the first of which is about me learning to drive.

At time of writing, I'm forty-eight years old and I still can't drive. Just between you and me, this is an ongoing source of shame. My driving instructor, a man with a neat moustache and aviator glasses, loved driving because he was obviously very good at it. He loved his car very much, and likewise the ins-and-outs of the Highway Code. He wasn't quite as keen on people who couldn't drive, by which I mean he didn't like learners, by which I mean he didn't like me.

The act of learning is challenging because learning is the ongoing status of *not* knowing something yet. *Not knowing* brings with it the inevitability of mistakes, and often, those mistakes will be made in front of other more experienced people. There is a public dimension to much of our formal learning, which is really quite unhelpful when you think about it, as most of us prefer to keep our respective pratfalls private.

Learning to drive felt very public indeed, with my lack of expertise monitored not just by the relative stranger sitting inches from me in the car, but by other motorists and passing pedestrians. As one driving lesson followed another, I realised I was getting on my instructor's nerves. I just wasn't very good at it. I wasn't quick on the up-take or 'a natural' and he and I both knew it.

Soon, instead of thinking about what I was supposed to be learning about driving, I started to worry much more about what my learning *looked like* to this other individual.

I worried, not about hill starts and zebra crossings, but about performing my learning in such a way as not to disappoint my instructor. Over time, my self-consciousness intensified, and all because I was acutely aware that I was learning in front of someone who knew more than me.

With learners and teachers, there is always someone in the room who has 'been there, done that', and on paper, this should be a relationship characterised by inspiration and reassurance. In my case, I was *more* resistant to learning *because* I was in the company of an expert.

So that's me aged seventeen, gripping the steering wheel rather miserably and failing, not just at driving, but at learning.

My second dinner party anecdote has me aged five or six and harbouring dreams of becoming a superhero and concluding that gymnastics is the closest I'll get to leaping tall buildings in a single bound.

I badgered my parents to enrol me in a local gymnastics club, but on the day of my very first class we arrived late, and I was mortified. I recall rushing in to find a throng of other children clad in white shorts and vests, merrily darting around the village hall. At that same moment, the instructor handed me a worksheet listing an array of gymnastic manoeuvres. Nowhere did the worksheet state, 'You should already be familiar with these exercises, and we expect you to perform them *perfectly*.' Nonetheless, that was my assumption and I'd made it because I'd arrived late and I was embarrassed. I assumed it because I'd missed the instructions.

I'd taken one glance at that formal-looking piece of paper and promptly decided that gymnastics wasn't for me after all. It couldn't be, could it? I couldn't execute any of the feats listed, and anyway, I was obviously nothing like these other more confident kids. I'd been foolish to think I could ever be a gymnast, let alone a superhero.

I fled the hall in tears, much to the bewilderment of my parents.

So why share these two uncomfortable and largely embarrassing stories in response to that dinner party query about why I chose to become a learning designer?

The truth is, whenever I design something for someone else to teach, these same two versions of myself - the boy who aspired to be a gymnast and the teenager who detested his driving lessons - they stand beside me, observing what I do with keen interest. It turns out that even when I was failing to learn gymnastics or how to parallel park, I was learning something after all. Turns out I was gaining really valuable insights into the barriers that exist in the minds of learners, regardless of what they're trying to grasp and regardless of their age.

It's likely every learner harbours a concern about how their level of expertise measures up to that of others. They're already fretting about the dynamic between themselves, the body of knowledge they've come to acquire, and the more knowledgeable others whose job it is to explain it. I think learners are anxious about a bunch of things that remain unseen, unspoken, and it's this hidden aspect of how we learn (and why we don't) that I find most interesting of all.

To learn is to be more exposed, more vulnerable, more 'out there' than before. Hence, for me, the act of learning design always commences with an act of recollection, and with efforts of imagination and empathy. To design learning effectively is to never forget what it's like to be someone who doesn't possess a particular knowledge, who isn't yet acquainted with the conventions of a specific discipline or institution, who hasn't yet encountered those special words, those integral concepts, those tacit customs.

So often, the true challenge of learning isn't rooted in what is difficult about the discipline itself, but in what is difficult about how we feel about acquiring it.

In my view, learning design hinges on a continual exercise of memory. The job is a constant effort of imagination and empathy. It's about perpetually remembering what it's like to be the individual *without* the expertise, *without* the experience, and it's within this 'knowledge of lack' that I believe some of our most important work as learning designers takes place.

"Phil's anecdotes remind us that every learner grapples with the fear of being exposed and vulnerable, feelings that often remain hidden beneath the surface of formal education.

As a learning designer, Phil's stories reinforce my belief in the pivotal role of empathy in effective learning design. It's crucial to continually exercise our imagination, placing ourselves in the shoes of learners who lack specific knowledge or are navigating unfamiliar concepts.

The essence of learning design lies not only in addressing the challenges of the subject matter but also in understanding the emotional aspects of the learner's journey.

Once we do this, we can begin anticipating and removing barriers that may prevent them from learning."

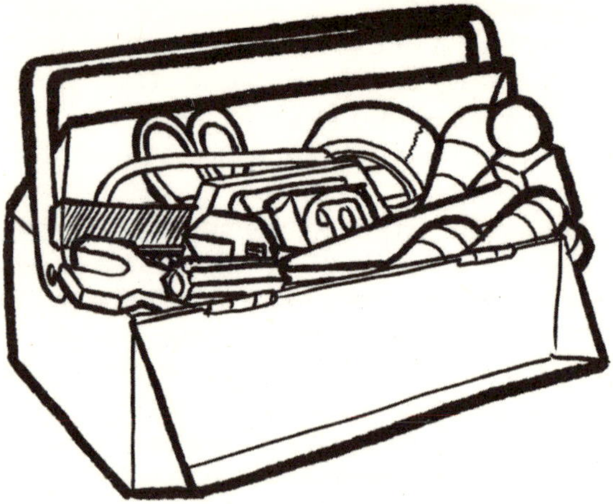

Ding's Toolkit

A surgeon has tools, a builder has tools. And theories are some of the most powerful tools a learning designer can use to build effective learning experiences.

Different learning designers will prefer different theories, and that's absolutely fine. The important thing is that a programme of formal learning is informed by one or more learning theories.

But why, we hear you ask? Aren't theories really abstract and boring?

Nope. Let us explain.

Learning is complex, and there is no single agreed definition of what learning *is*, or how it happens. This is why there are many different theories about how we learn.

Some theories are highly practical, and some are more conceptual. But every learning theory provides us with a way of understanding how to design effective learning experiences.

Look out for Ding's Toolkit in the following pages, where we'll highlight some learning theories and how they can help you design and build with confidence.

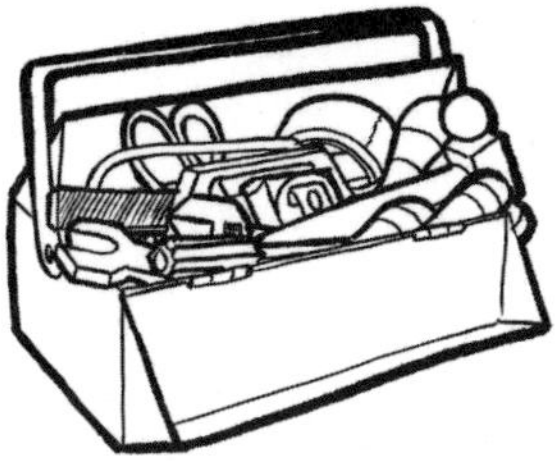

Ding's Toolbox: Empathy

Renowned psychologist **Carl Rogers** advocated understanding and accepting clients' communications. Similarly, in teaching and designing, comprehending learners' backgrounds enhances engagement. It's about accepting them as they are, not as you wish them to be. Genuine empathy allows for tough conversations without feeling like a personal attack. This is 'unconditional positive regard'. For learning designers, empathy is your most potent tool. It unlocks doors, removes barriers, and inspires inclusive, transformative learning.

Instructions for Use:

1. **Deep Understanding:** Step into the learner's shoes to identify their hurdles, from confidence gaps to task completion worries.
2. **Tailored Design:** Craft your learning experience with the learner's unique challenges in mind. This ensures a more impactful and relevant course.
3. **Trust Building:** Use empathy to have tough conversations with care and respect. Establish 'unconditional positive regard' to foster trust and transformation.

Key Benefits:

- **Breaks Barriers:** Empathy uncovers hidden obstacles, paving the way for smoother learning experiences.
- **Enhanced Engagement:** Learners feel understood and valued, leading to increased motivation and participation.
- **Customised Learning:** Design courses that truly meet learners where they are, fostering a more inclusive environment.
- **Trust and Transformation:** Build trust through empathy, enabling meaningful conversations that drive genuine growth.

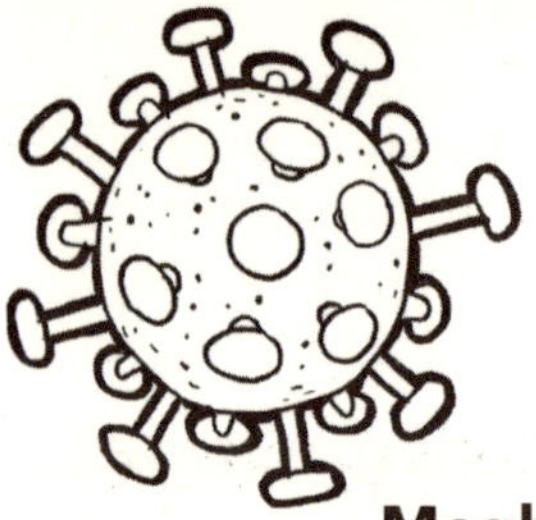

Ding's Covid Diaries:
Meghana Bisineer Part 2, January 2021

Insights from a year of teaching remotely

It's been an interesting semester, to say the least! Teaching online has presented its challenges, but there have been some unexpected positives. The students have shown incredible resilience and adaptability. Particularly, the first-year students who, despite not physically being on campus, have shown enthusiasm and excitement for learning.

Then there are the senior students, who took a bit longer to adjust. They're more aware of what they're missing out on, but they've still managed to rise to the occasion. The key difference I've noticed is that the seniors have a strong support network within their cohort, while the first-years are still getting to know each other.

As for the online platforms, I've kept it fairly simple with Moodle for course materials, Zoom for virtual classes, and VoiceThread for assignments. It's been a learning curve for everyone, including me, but I've been pleasantly surprised at how quickly everyone adapted to these platforms.

Creating a sense of community has been a bit more challenging. I've had to rely on smaller critique groups and other strategies to facilitate connections among the students. It's not quite the same as the in-person experience, but we're making the best of it.

The most surprising aspect of this transition has been how well the students have responded to the online format. They've shown an impressive level of engagement and creativity, even without the physical studio space. I've had to adjust my teaching style, making sure to provide clear instructions and demos. It's a lot more preparation on my end, but it's paying off in terms of the quality of work they're producing.

Regarding the time difference, it's been a significant adjustment. I'm teaching from 8 p.m. to 3 a.m. due to the time zone difference between the UK and California. It's a bit unconventional, but it's what works for the students, and they've been very appreciative of the effort.

As for avoiding burnout, it's been a challenge. There have been moments when both the students and I have felt the strain. The external factors, like the ongoing pandemic and other global events, certainly add to the stress. I've tried to be understanding and flexible, while also maintaining academic standards.

One thing that's become clear is the importance of clear communication and detailed instructions. I've had to create demo videos and provide ample examples and inspiration for assignments. It's a different approach from what I'd do in a physical classroom, but it's working.

Overall, while there have been challenges, there have also been some unexpected benefits to teaching online. It's forced me to think creatively about how to maintain a sense of community and engagement in a virtual setting. And it's shown me just how resilient and adaptable both the students and I can be.

Ding's Hot Takeaway: Mitigating Burn-Out #1

Burn-out: *a state of chronic physical and emotional exhaustion often resulting from prolonged periods of excessive stress, demanding work, or overwhelming responsibilities.*

Burn-out is characterised by feelings of fatigue, cynicism, and a reduced sense of personal accomplishment. Individuals experiencing burn-out may find it challenging to meet the demands of their work or daily life, leading to a decline in productivity, motivation, and overall well-being.

Here are five key takeaways for mitigating burnout **for educators** through effective learning design:

1. **Manageable Workloads:** Design courses with a realistic workload, avoiding excessive assignments and administrative tasks.
2. **Clear Course Outlines:** Provide well-structured course outlines with learning objectives, assessment details, and a clear timeline to help educators plan effectively.
3. **Flexible Teaching Methods:** Allow for a variety of teaching approaches to accommodate different preferences and strengths, empowering educators in their teaching style.
4. **Balanced Technology Integration:** Offer training and support with digital technologies to ensure they enhance rather than overwhelm the teaching experience.
5. **Community and Support:** Foster a sense of community among educators, encouraging collaboration, resource-sharing, and mentorship opportunities.

Ding's Hot Takeaway: Mitigating Burn-Out #2

Here are five key tips to mitigate burnout **for learners** through effective learning design:

1. **Clear Learning Objectives:** Ensure that learners understand what is expected of them in each module or session, providing a clear sense of direction and purpose.
2. **Varied Learning Resources:** Offer a diverse range of content types to keep learners engaged and prevent monotony, including videos, articles, interactive exercises, and discussions.
3. **Self-paced Learning:** Allow learners to progress at their own speed, accommodating different learning styles and reducing unnecessary pressure.
4. **Supportive Learning Community:** Foster opportunities for interaction with peers, creating a sense of community, providing motivation, and reducing feelings of isolation.
5. **Constructive Feedback and Realistic Milestones:** Provide timely, specific feedback and break down larger tasks into manageable milestones, preventing learners from becoming overwhelmed.

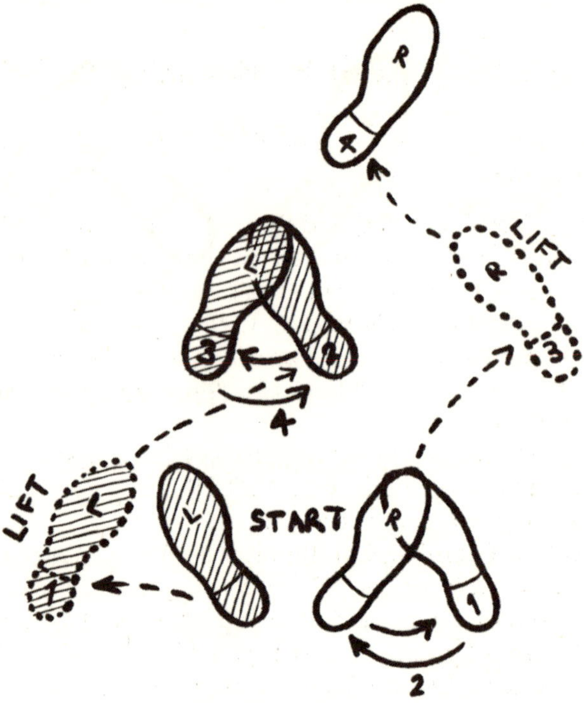

Ding's Learning Design Manoeuvres

When it comes to being a successful learning designer you need to be adaptable, imaginative and fleet-of-foot.

Ding has gathered together some really effective learning design manoeuvres and we'll be sharing them in the following pages. Positions please!

The Virtual Campfire

A 'virtual campfire' is a metaphorical term used to describe online spaces or activities that facilitate community, connection, and meaningful interaction among individuals, particularly in virtual or remote settings. The term draws on the imagery of gathering around a campfire, a traditional setting for storytelling, sharing experiences, and building a sense of camaraderie.

In an educational context, virtual campfires can be created through various digital platforms and strategies to replicate the sense of community and engagement that might be fostered in a physical classroom. This can include virtual discussion forums, video conferences, collaborative projects, or other online activities that encourage participants to share their thoughts, experiences, and ideas.

The aim of virtual campfires is to provide a space for participants to connect on a personal and intellectual level, fostering a sense of belonging and mutual support. This is particularly important in remote learning environments, where physical distance can sometimes lead to a sense of isolation.

Overall, virtual campfires are a creative way to design online learning experiences that prioritise community building, interaction, and the sharing of knowledge and experiences. They help to mitigate the potential feelings of disconnection and burnout that can arise in virtual or remote educational settings.

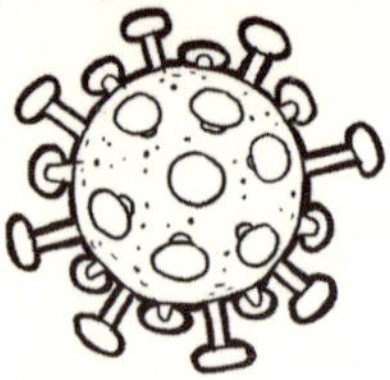

Ding's Covid Diaries:

Santa Hat Friday, Phil Gomm, December 2020

Not unlike the little match girl in the well-known festive fairy story, I find myself looking into the dark shuttered interiors of our Tier 3 pubs, wishing for happier times. I feel for all the publicans right now and worry about all the little dark spots that have opened up in people's lives where a pint and packet of crisps once shone.

As a former licensee myself, I have never been confused about the real value of a pub or bar to its community. I was probably happiest when I was running a bar; knowing the exact moment to dim the lights or dial up the volume to bring about some deepening of the social interactions taking place before me; knowing how something as simple as remembering someone's name and their preferred drink in their preferred glass could both settle and ennoble them. I recall fondly all the small ways in which proximity and a lovely bit of buzz would see friendship groups diversify and move towards unexpected and unpredictable intimacies. I remember what it was like to produce the conditions for the making of companions from strangers.

When I look into the pub windows, discarded face masks blowing about my feet like leaves, I ache for my barkeep-self, who was younger certainly, who worried less, who could drink eight espressos and sleep like a log.

I think too of my other former job role, as course leader for an undergraduate arts degree. Despairing at all those empty chairs and tables, I repopulate them with rose-tinted memories of evenings spent in UK pubs and European bars in the company of my students, alumni, and staff. In these vignettes, we are imbibing gaudy glasses of Aperol Spritz in the lobby of a down-at-heel Roman hotel and sipping mojitos in some gorgeous dive in the labyrinthine heart of La Rambla. In other memories, we are sitting around the sticky, dark wood tables of a Kent boozer, sporting Poundland hats in the shape of Christmas puddings.

Back then, 'Santa Hat Friday' was an annual festive rite, seeing staff, students, and alumni convene in our local for an end-of-term wind-down. While not mandatory, the wearing of seasonally-inspired hats was encouraged (in truth, very little encouragement was required). After the very last hand-in, after the long hard slog of the autumn term, we would amble down to the Highstreet, making for a colourful, if untidy, ribbon of revellers.

But it would be a mistake to presume there was anything instinctive about this community of ours looking to spend a night out together as the natural extension of some shared existing culture or innate behaviour. This course tradition had to be enacted. Many of my students suffered with acute social anxiety. A higher-than-average proportion of their number were neuro-diverse in variously wonderful ways. They likewise came in every shade of the LGBTQ+ rainbow. My students were black, and they were brown, multi-faith and studying with us from overseas. There were students who had never once frequented a public house, students who didn't drink, and growing numbers of undergraduates who saw 'the pub' as a rather strange, pointless, and provincial space, lacking both the insulation and connectivity of their preferred social media platforms.

For these reasons, 'Santa Hat Friday' presented a challenge. More cautious members of academic staff on other courses, and some of those among the ranks of student welfare, raised their eyebrows at the propriety of this extracurricular activity. Was it appropriate to organise course-based events in which some students might feel less able to participate? Was I engineering a scenario wherein some members of my course community might feel isolated, othered, or coerced? Indeed, was it even *seemly* for course staff to accompany their young wards to the pub, and worse still, while wearing a jaunty pair of flashing antlers?

I used to roll my eyes at all the hand-wringing. For an event like this to achieve such contrary ambitions, the community leader organising it would need to have the EQ of a mince pie. I approached this extra-curricular activity as I approached every other course-related opportunity for the empowerment of a disparate group of young people, who, for all the reasons described above, might experience social disadvantage were they to continue worrying about engaging with noisier, less pastoral, less well-regulated spaces. I felt it important to actually produce the conditions under which less naturally confident students would actively struggle, in the knowledge they were safe to struggle because the rest of us were there too; in the knowledge that 'struggle' is a half-way house enroute to something valuable, lasting and new.

Every Santa Hat Friday was a short bonus module in fostering employability - and no, I am not talking about the awful hollowed-out sense of the word that narrows the value of higher education to only its most immediate relevance to some industry or other. I'm talking instead about a young person's cognisance of, and confidence in, following (and resisting!), the unwritten rules of the communal workplace and beyond. I'm talking about their literacy in the unspoken languages of the graduate marketplace. I am talking about growing their power.

So, when I find myself standing outside these shuttered pubs, reminiscing about Santa Hat Friday and other ghosts of Christmas past, I'm not feeling sorry for myself, though I'm not above admitting how much I miss large elements of my former life, principally that colourful, untidy ribbon of students, alumni and staff I had the very real privilege of working alongside for ten years or so. Neither am I pining for my days as a licensee, when the cuffs of every white shirt I owned were liver-spotted with Guinness, and I smelled powerfully of cigarette smoke from dawn 'til dusk. What I'm really thinking about is the impact of COVID on the student experience – not as it pertains to the National Student Survey, or 'value for money', or their rights as consumers (yawn) – but as it relates to their opportunities to learn invaluable skills from the rough and tumble of more disorderly spaces.

And while I'm in this nostalgic mood, I might kid myself my former students learned everything of real and lasting importance from the content of my lectures... but I know very well, if surveyed, they'd more likely talk about their field trip to Berlin, to Prague, to Barcelona, to Rome. They would recall squeezing into dimly-lit hostels, exhausted after early starts and awful flights, negotiating the complex unwritten rules of allocating bunk beds. They'd pick nights out in crappy clubs, where they spoke, for the first time, to a classmate they'd otherwise always avoided, or judged, or envied, or fancied. They might point at some group photograph taken on the worn stone steps of some ancient feat of classical architecture, in which young people from a multiplicity of backgrounds all look as deliriously sleep-deprived as each other. Some of them might even have a fond thing to say about those Santa Hat Fridays, about what it feels like to be part of a community of practice, to feel it binding so reassuringly about you.

In my new role working alongside Dr Tony Reeves at Ding, I'm talking with amazing tutors who have adapted to the new normal of online learning with imagination and dexterity. I have nothing but admiration for the different ways in which tutors have safeguarded their student communities during this hugely challenging time. But as I stand reflected in these gloomy pub windows, thinking how ridiculous I must have looked in my Christmas Pudding hat, I worry more and more about all the little dark spots opening up in the student experience, and I'm keen to understand what more we could be doing to light them back up.

"You know, Tony, sometimes I get the feeling my students probably remember the field trips more vividly than they do any of my riveting lectures. It's a good thing, of course, but it makes me wonder about the weight we place on academic content..."

"Ha, I can totally relate, Phil. It's like they remember the dodgy hostel in Berlin over our meticulously crafted PowerPoints! But you know what? I think there's a deeper truth there. Experiences, especially the ones that take them out of their comfort zones, tend to stick. It's not about side-lining academic content, but recognising that learning isn't confined to the classroom."

"Absolutely, Tony. Those experiences are like imprints, etched in their memories. It's got me thinking - shouldn't we be weaving more of these into the curriculum? I mean, imagine if the learning experiences were as vivid and impactful as those field trips."

"It's about striking a balance. Academic content provides the foundation, but these extracurricular experiences, they're the sparks that light the fire of real learning. They offer context, application, and sometimes, even inspiration."

"So true, Tony. It's not just about knowledge transfer; it's about application and understanding in the real world. But how do we go about integrating these experiences into our curriculum without overwhelming the students?"

"That's the challenge, isn't it? Learning design needs to be intentional. It's about identifying key moments where these experiences can enhance the learning. Field trips, workshops, collaborative projects – they should be purposeful extensions of what we teach. And let's not forget reflection. That's where the real gold of experiential learning is unearthed. We're not just designing lessons; we're orchestrating experiences. That is where true learning happens."

Ray's Story

My transition into teaching didn't come from a burning passion to educate; it was more about wanting to help people. Sitting in an office didn't quite do it.

My first teaching job was the right opportunity: an international sixth form college with students far from home in a remote part of the countryside (and perishing cold for many of them for much of the time). I loved the 'looking after' and found there too that I felt passionate about learning. I began to do courses in study skills (so new, almost no one had heard of such a thing), in developing self-esteem, self-confidence and work/life balance.

And somewhere in the byways, I found dyslexia – again, so new, almost no one knew about it. This took me into Higher Education, on to inclusive practice and into teaching teachers.

The core beliefs remain: the importance of inclusivity, social justice, 'state', empathy, caring (Nel Noddings is a hero), the whole person – and supporting students, old and young, to become 'aware of themselves and their potential in a world that is open, fluid, contested and in need of courageous actions'.

I fidget around moral education and the loss of Ethics from curriculums and am with Gert Biesta (another hero) in believing 'the educational gesture must remain hesitant and gentle'

Then there's fun – fun is fundamental, and, like Renoir on painting, I wouldn't do it if it wasn't enjoyable.

Rays Of Light

Rays Of Light is our very own problem-page-come-help-desk, staffed by Ding's doyenne of inclusivity, Ray Martin.

Ray's postbag is always chockful of questions from educators and learning designers as to how they might ensure the design and delivery of their learning resources is as inclusive as possible. Ray is always on hand to offer great advice and practical suggestions.

Look out for Ray's illuminations throughout this edition of Ding's Almanac.

Dear Ray,

I've been working on course design lately, and I want to ensure it caters to dyspraxic students. It's a real challenge, and I'd love your advice on how to go about it effectively.

Asmee, Leamington Spa

Dear Asmee,

Thank you for your letter. You're definitely heading in the right direction by considering the needs of dyspraxic students. Remember, what benefits them often benefits everyone. Here are some practical tips:

1.Clarity is Key: Clear learning objectives upfront and at the end of sessions help everyone, not just dyspraxic learners, to grasp the bigger picture.

2.Bite-sized Instructions: Keep tasks in small, manageable chunks. It's easier to process and avoids overloading working memory.

3.Breaks Matter: Short, regular breaks are a lifesaver. They give everyone a chance to recharge and maintain focus.

4.Early Access to Material: Providing notes and handouts beforehand aids preparation and understanding, which benefits all students.

5.Embrace Repetition: Practice makes perfect, especially for dyspraxic learners. Over-learning is key to mastery.

And remember, praise effort over outcome. This small shift can make a world of difference. Keep up the good work!

Warm regards, Ray

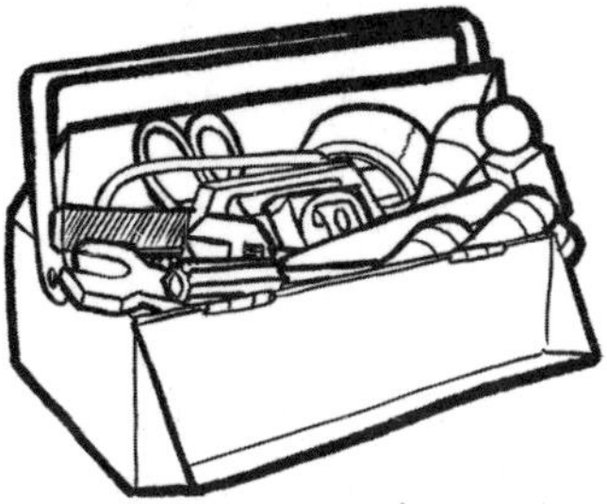

Ding's Toolbox: The Hidden Curriculum

Just as invisible ink only reveals its message under specific conditions, the 'hidden curriculum' comprises unspoken values, norms and behaviours in an educational setting. Implicit criteria for evaluating learning can adversely affect some students. Learning designers shape the curriculum, deciding what to include; their conversations with subject matter experts are vital for uncovering implicit biases.

For example, while planning a data management course, the subject matter expert keeps emphasising the need for commercial awareness, professionalism, and collaboration – even though these skills are not represented by the more data-specific learning outcomes identified by the SME!

Using the Hidden Curriculum as an Inclusivity Tool:

Step 1: Identify Content and Implicit Factors

- List subject-specific content for learning.
- Compile other crucial factors <u>not</u> part of the curriculum.

Step 2: Assess Benefits and Risks

- Briefly outline advantages and drawbacks of including these factors.

Step 3: Refine Learning Outcomes

- Adjust intended learning outcomes based on the assessment.

Using the Hidden Curriculum as an inclusivity tool empowers learning designers to create fair and effective learning environments. By addressing implicit biases and expectations, we ensure inclusivity for all learners.

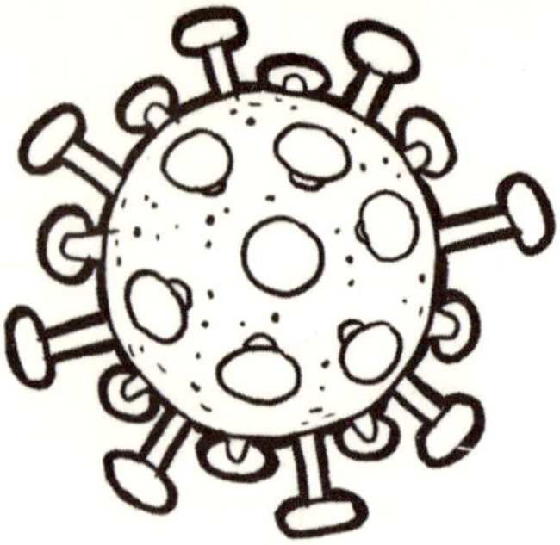

Ding's Covid Diaries:
Allan Atlee, September 2020

How creative higher education is responding to Covid

Over the past year, I've been witness to a remarkable transformation in the landscape of art and design education. The abrupt shift to online learning, catalysed by the COVID-19 pandemic, brought about a set of challenges that were particularly distinct to our field.

In the realm of art and design, our traditional approach is steeped in the tactile, hands-on experience of studio work. Students typically flow freely between workshops and studios, nurturing a dynamic and interactive learning environment. However, this natural rhythm was disrupted by the transition to online learning. Recreating the impromptu encounters and unscripted guidance that define our pedagogy proved to be a formidable task.

As educators, we had to pivot swiftly. Some of our colleagues, especially those well-versed in digital pedagogy, navigated this transition seamlessly. However, for many art and design institutions, including ours, there was a learning curve. We leaned heavily on the expertise of a select few digital pedagogues, who graciously shared their experiences and hard-earned insights. We swiftly recognised the value of structure in online learning, providing clear touchpoints for students to engage and reflect.

Peer-to-peer learning, which is the lifeblood of studio environments, needed to be reimagined. It was imperative to create spaces for students to connect, share, and engage in meaningful discussions. Granting students access to technicians in casual, virtual settings aimed to replicate the organic interactions they would have experienced on campus.

Curiously, online learning brought forth an unexpected boon. It fostered deeper connections between students and their tutors. The structured one-on-one tutorials, even though conducted through screens, provided a platform for students to be heard more attentively and build more profound relationships with their tutors. This shift was particularly beneficial for introverted and contemplative students.

Moreover, it underscored the urgency of addressing matters of diversity and inclusion in higher education. The events of the past years, including the impassioned calls of the Black Lives Matter movement and the escalating climate crisis, have spurred us to re-evaluate our approaches. Students are rightfully demanding swift action, compelling us to reflect deeply on how we can forge a more equitable and inclusive learning environment.

Over the past year, our approach to education has seen a significant transformation. While we were more understanding of students' circumstances and their impact on learning, our bureaucratic and technocratic processes were sometimes barriers, especially for those facing unique challenges in their personal lives. We've become more generous in allowing diverse expressions of learning in assessments.

In the realm of art and design education, there has been a shift in our perspective on assessment. It's no longer just about the end product; we now recognise the student as the central focus. This shift demands a truly inclusive approach to assessment, going beyond considerations of hardship or access to resources.

Moreover, we've come to understand that assessment extends beyond the tangible. It encompasses the mindset and cultural position of each student and how they choose to convey their learning. This calls for a greater willingness to accept diverse forms of evidence for learning.

In tutorials, we're careful to ensure that what we perceive as 'a laid-back approach' to pedagogy doesn't inadvertently perpetuate existing privileges. We've become attuned to the fact that students from different backgrounds may experience the learning environment differently.

Equality and access to learning resources are paramount considerations. This isn't just a temporary response to COVID-19; it's a commitment to an inclusive future. Extending hardship funds to support students lacking technology or facing time and space constraints has been a step in the right direction.

The online learning environment, while offering a potentially more egalitarian space, also brings its own challenges. Disparities in internet connectivity and living conditions can pose significant obstacles.

Moving forward, in this post-COVID era, designing courses and learning programmes requires a bespoke approach. Learning begins with the individual student, and courses and assessments should be tailored accordingly. The recent controversy surrounding algorithms in education underscores the importance of thoughtful, nuanced assessment.

The events of the past year have compelled us to re-evaluate our approach to education. This includes a shift in how we view assessment, a commitment to inclusivity, and a recognition of the diverse circumstances in which our students learn.

As we navigate this new normal, a student-centred, inclusive, and flexible approach to learning and assessment will be key to ensuring the success of all students.

Ding's Hot Takeaways
from Allan Atlee's Covid experience

1. **Swift Evolution of Learning:** The pandemic accelerated changes already in the pipeline. Learning designers must remain nimble, ready to pivot and innovate as education continues to transform.
2. **Distinct Challenges in Creative Disciplines:** The practical nature of art and design education posed unique hurdles online. Learning designers must craft immersive virtual experiences that nurture creativity and collaboration, addressing the absence of physical workshops.
3. **Balancing Virtual Engagement:** Online learning offers intimate interactions, yet maintaining a sense of community is crucial. Learning designers must prioritise strategies fostering peer interactions and group dynamics to sustain student engagement.
4. **Promoting Equity and Inclusion:** Virtual learning accentuated access disparities. Learning designers should forge courses catering to diverse backgrounds, ensuring every student enjoys equal opportunities for success.
5. **Shift towards Transformative Education:** The pandemic spurred a rethinking of educational objectives, spotlighting inclusivity, empathy, and transformative experiences. Learning designers should emphasise comprehensive assessment methods and blended learning approaches, equipping students for an ever-changing world.

Fierce Grinding Discords:

on student dissatisfaction and the responsibilities of listening

All these years later, I'm still haunted by a 1981 episode of the television series, *Tales Of The Unexpected*. Entitled *The Sound Machine*, and adapted from a Roald Dahl short story, the episode introduces us to Klausner, an enthusiast of sound;

"I believe ... there is a whole world of sound about us all the time that we cannot hear. It is possible that up there in those high-pitched inaudible regions there is a new exciting music being made, with subtle harmonies and fierce grinding discords, a music so powerful that it would drive us mad if only our ears were tuned to hear the sound of it."

In pursuit of his ambition to apprehend sounds undetectable to the normal range of human hearing, Klausner invents a listening device. At first, Klausner doesn't understand the provenance of the screams detected by his machine when he tests his apparatus out in his garden - until he notices his neighbour snipping the blooms from her rose bush. Klausner's sound machine is hearing the agonies of plants!

As a child, this episode did for walking across lawns what *Jaws* did for the deep end of my local swimming pool, freighting ubiquitous behaviours in familiar environments with new probabilities of risk. These days, I'm more likely to worry about entire ecosystems than the discomfort experienced by the few blades of grass between my toes. Even so, I still find myself thinking about Klausner's sound machine, and the act of listening to pain.

Given the clear and obvious impact of the pandemic on student well-being, and on the institutional infrastructures in place to support it, discussions around the responsibility for the pastoral care of undergraduates have intensified. Even before the advent of Covid, the term 'epidemic' was much used to characterise the rise of poor mental health among university students.

In my previous institution, initiatives to support student well-being proliferated like plucky mushrooms. There were 'listening posts' and 'Mood Boost' workshops and online counselling sessions, hopelessly over-subscribed. Consider our incessant hand-wringing over the ethics of granting extenuating circumstances to students, with the university unable to make up its mind as to whether the glass was half-full or half-empty, when it came to recording high numbers of extended deadlines and interruptions of study. Was making extensions available to ever-growing numbers of undergraduates indicative of greater inclusivity, and welcome move towards student-centred learning? Or proof instead of systemic course-level failure? By seeking out extra time and additional allowances, were students demonstrating commendable levels of self-determination, or just vapid snowflakes, melting wetly, the institution wilting similarly under the glare of its canny customers?

When the conservative government cut funding for disabled students in higher education, there were those in the university who feared the good and proper project of widening participation would now continue in name only, in service to the institution's recruitment targets and not much else. For others, the paring back of learning support assistants and free laptops was like being given permission to switch off an expensive machine that was keeping the pipe-dreams alive of students otherwise ill-suited to the rigours of higher education.

Sometimes, often, I'd hear colleagues talking about 'the good old days', when undergraduates just *knew* how to study; when they were resilient, self-directed, arriving on day one of year one as savvy, professionalised learners. Hand-on-heart, I wasn't immune to prelapsarian thoughts myself, dog-tired after another round of tutorials with unhappy students. But golden ageism is always bullshit, as we know very well. We might look back wistfully at tutors from yesteryear going about their simpler business in their simpler classrooms with their simpler cohorts, just as Klausner might once have smiled fondly at someone taking their shears to a hedge. We might coo nostalgically over all those seemingly stoic undergraduates, the sort who "bloody well just got on with it"; strong, silent types, who could be relied upon to metabolise gumption from hardship.

But let's imagine, in addition to its existing functions, Klausner's sound machine has the capacity to detect the frequencies of the past, and how about we turn the dial: what's that I hear? Ah yes, it is those same fierce grinding discords, the as-of-now unmuted miseries of diverse groups of individuals being nicked, bruised, picked at, and broken by the everyday habits of teachers and the mono-cultures of their classrooms; and not injuries inflicted on purpose, not always anyway, but injuries nonetheless.

When I think back to the classrooms of my own secondary modern, my blood runs cold in the knowledge of this parallel universe of suffering, rendered undetectable by the deficit in my own perceptual apparatus. I remember the rather odd-seeming children hidden away at the back of the class who wouldn't meet your eye, whose non sequiturs disrupted the teacher's flow and magnetised the bullies. I recall the clamour of the disruptive boys, too quick and too clever to know when to wind in their necks, but too 'stupid' to read the black board; and I think about the weird kids, the whey-faced loners standing disconsolately at the edge of the playground, friendless inside the hoods of their parkas.

These young people were all unheard and unhearable in their different ways, for how to detect the call-to-action of Asperger's when it's carried by a frequency to which no one is yet attuned? How to decipher the dissonance of dyslexia when the only sound it makes in the world of other people is naughtiness?

How to mitigate against acute social anxiety, when there is insufficient bandwidth by which to detect it?

But that was then, the 'good old days', when all the stupid, damaged people knew better than to go to university, when silence was golden...

The good news is most universities are packing impressive sound devices now, installed and finely calibrated in the service of retention and the closing of attainment gaps, and if not quite that, then grimly determined to deliver on decent student satisfaction scores and value for money. We are encouraged to detect and manage the emotional well-being of students earlier and earlier, to guard against their unhappiness, or even worse, them going somewhere else and taking their fees with them.

During my stint as course leader, I was having more and more conversations with students about their private pain and its impact on their studies. I encountered students who didn't want to write anything because the prospect of writing made them too uncomfortable; and students who didn't want to talk in front of their peers, work in groups or give presentations because the prospect of doing so triggered their anxiety. I once supported a student who didn't like experiencing feelings of 'suspense', so excused themselves from watching films that were 'suspenseful'. Institutionally, I began to see a reciprocal trend for clearing the path of obstacles between students and their degree awards, born of all our enlightened acts of listening. I witnessed word counts shrinking, and the reshaping of curricula and credit frameworks, and alluring debates around alternative assessment gaining more and more ground with senior management.

If Klausner happened to wave his sound machine in *my* direction, he would have heard me screaming inside. In common with many of my colleagues, academic and otherwise, I was becoming increasingly uneasy at all the listening - but not because I was measuring my fabulously diverse student cohorts against paragons of resilience from some imagined rose-tinted past.

At the conclusion of *The Sound Machine*, Klausner, fully sensate to the hitherto ignored feelings of the flora surrounding him, insists a doctor applies iodine to an axe wound in an oak tree. As sensitised to the feelings of our student bodies, we've come to similarly rely on the various student support services in place to soothe them. Equipped now with our own sound machines, we know how to better detect the tell-tale frequencies emitted by anxiety disorders and neuro-diversity, and we know what to do about it; *refer, refer, refer*: "Go to the VLE and download the policy on applying for an extension"; "Go get a doctor's note in support of your claim"; "Go make an appointment with the counsellor." Go, go, *go!*

All of which looks responsible, commendable, best practice even, until I remind myself, in *The Sound Machine* story, it was Klausner who first hit the tree with the axe.

While I always worked closely and collaboratively with student support services, I was keenly interested in understanding what might be producing all this pain in the first place. What point, I wondered, to all this listening, if we dedicate ourselves to reacting to the resonances of the wounded, and never to the swing of the axe? And while, I hope, I was an academic far removed from the tone-deaf tutors of the golden age of education, I wondered if there was still more I could do pre-emptively and began by assuming there was.

Sure, this quest was driven by my interest in producing transformative learning experiences for each and every individual under my care, but it was fired too by bone-deep exasperation at giving so much of my time and energy to pastoral emergencies. Oh, for a day without another student panic attack! Oh, for a unit submission *without* the accompanying confetti of exemptions.

You might say I was dreaming again of a life of silence, and not the bad old kind of the good old days, but the hush produced by higher frequencies of student contentment.

Just as *The Sound Machine* episode provoked my boyhood self into re-looking at seemingly benign environments for probabilities of risk, I turned my attentions to thinking about the design and delivery of year one of my particular degree programme. I was looking for axes, the glint of things we were doing badly. I looked for cruelties and insensitivity, for any unfair exclusionary practices.

I didn't find any concealed weapons in our learning aims and outcomes, but as a first-year tutor myself, I was able to cut through to something important, to an idea as bold-seeming as it was likely obvious, and it was this: the teaching on first year programmes should not be modelled after the image of the first-year undergraduate you *hope* is coming to study with you, but instead, after the image of the sort of second year student you want your first-year programme to *produce*.

If we want second years (and thus third years, and thus graduates) unfazed by research and writing, unfazed by public-speaking and collaboration, and by the giving and receipt of constructive criticism, we need to stop anticipating these skills from our first-years to ensure we're actually *teaching* these skills to our first-years. We need to situate their worries as normal and appropriate, to design *for* them - and not to shame them, anaesthetise them, aggrandise them, or remove them, but to overt them to convert them.

When I asked myself what an undergraduate course without discomfort might look like, I shuddered. To return to *The Sound Machine*'s image of the neighbour cutting her rose bush, it is also true that expert and judicious pruning produces more flowers. Pruning excises old wood and triggers new growth, but thanks to Klausner's sound machine, we also know this intervention is painful for its subject.

When I listened too long to Heads of School, or listened too long to certain student reps, I felt we were in danger of advocating for lobotomies, for excising the pain centres from our learners' brains, as a sure-fire way to keep them smiling.

I began to feel as if our institutional sound machines, for all their good intentions, were producing the effect of deafness in tutors themselves, a growing inability to distinguish our prime responsibilities to students, as educators, from the white noise produced by the effect of aggressive marketisation on our understanding of student satisfaction.

I feared I was witnessing the activity of listening being co-opted into damaging long-term strategies for the nullification of short-term dissatisfaction, to the detriment of inclusivity and social mobility. By roping off certain types of academic or social activity from certain profiles of student, I worried we were only re-silencing their future selves. I knew very well that reading and writing, presenting and group work produced spikes of anxiety in many of my students. I wanted to see their anxiety managed *by* them, so not by removing its source, but instead by teaching into these challenging subjects imaginatively, creatively, inclusively, brilliantly. These were discomforts I *wanted* for my students because, to overcome them was to learn, to change, to transform; to expose their impermanence; to laugh at fear now and forever after; to win.

I understand it's confusing.

It sounds suddenly as if I have something in common with those former colleagues, who believed students should just 'bloody well get on with it', but that is not the gong I'm banging. Resilience is the weasel word for expecting people to get on with things uncomplainingly because they shouldn't hope for better; instead of being angry at baked-in injustice, they should knuckle-down and pull themselves up.

But I'm not confused at all.

The drum I'm banging sounds like this:

Begin by making different assumptions about your incoming first-year students. While they've elected to study with you, they are more reluctant than they're letting on. They will show resistance. They will avoid engaging with activities that worry them the most. This seems like a contradiction or a character flaw, but it isn't. You can want what scares you, and you can know the value of a thing even as you put your energies into avoiding it.

You might not be able to detect the background hum of first-year distress, perhaps because your own familiarity with the rituals of higher education and the foibles of your institution have left you a bit hard of hearing. As Klausner's sound machine teaches us, just because you can't hear something doesn't mean it's not making a noise. And while first-year students are worried by the prospect of learning new things, they are as worried, even more so, by the idea of confronting all the old things they've *always* found difficult or discomforting; perhaps because, before they met you, they sat in classrooms not dissimilar to the ones of my memory, classrooms without any sound machines in them at all.

In the new knowledge your first-years, a) don't already know how to do what you want them to do, and b) feel put at risk at the prospect of trying to do it, you need to, c) teach all of them how to do all of the things you regard as vital for undergraduates. Then, d) keep explaining why what you're teaching them is valuable, and e) teach those things in ways calibrated to reframe anxiety, not as an expression of weakness or dysfunction, but as a normal frequency of learning.

When you design and deliver programmes of study for first-years, as first-years actually *are*, your teaching will still discomfort, unsettle and provoke students. You are in the business of pruning roses, and the cries of students must be borne by everyone, by the student, by the tutor, and by the institution, as this dissatisfaction is the short-term noise produced by lasting, long-term change.

But if you don't design and deliver programmes of study for first-years as they actually are, (maybe because you can't remember what it's like to be one yourself, or don't care, or don't approve of first-years as they actually are), your teaching will be very painful. If you don't teach first-years how to do all the things you expect them to know how to do, and you don't explain your reasons why learning to do those things is important, (and then you fail them for not knowing how to do it or even caring about not knowing how to do it), you are not in the business of pruning roses, you are wielding an axe.

Referring your student to the counsellor, on account of their resulting panic attacks, is little different to sending a 'disruptive' child to sit at the back of the classroom with the other broken kids, whose own faults it must be they are too different, or too sad, or too angry to make a success of their learning. And if you're content to wield axes while bemoaning the spiralling culture of extenuating circumstances plaguing higher education, you must have your fingers in your ears, because the dissonance of that is deafening.

Discomforts like these should not be borne by students.

Discomforts like these should be acted upon by the institution, but I absolutely do not mean institutions should act by seeking to excise, reduce or demonise the learning activities that so predictably inflame the pain centres of students. I absolutely do not mean that all the difficult and challenging things we want our undergraduates to master should be removed from them because they produce discomfort.

I do not want lobotomies for learners. Instead, I want institutions to listen to what their sound machines are *really* detecting when it comes to the dissonance of student dissatisfaction. It's not the wailing of the evermore sick and the evermore stupid, or some klaxon calling time on what is 'too difficult for some' about higher learning, but a fierce and powerful clamour for truly inclusive curriculum design and its delivery for all.

Ding's Hot Takeaways
from Fierce Grinding Discords

1. **Reframe Assumptions About First-Year Students:** Instead of expecting first-year students to already possess certain skills, assume they may be unfamiliar with them and might feel apprehensive about trying. Design courses to teach these skills and explain their value, framing anxiety as a normal part of learning.
2. **Create Inclusive Curriculum Design:** Embrace the idea of inclusive curriculum design that accommodates a diverse range of students. This involves providing varied learning resources, clear instructions, and breaks, while also offering support services for those who may need them.
3. **Value Discomfort as a Catalyst for Growth:** Recognise that discomfort in learning can be a sign of transformative growth. Instead of removing challenging aspects of education, work to teach into them imaginatively and inclusively. Encourage students to confront and overcome these challenges, fostering resilience and adaptability.
4. **Listen Actively to Student Feedback:** Pay attention to the signals of dissatisfaction, not as a sign of failure, but as an opportunity for positive change in curriculum design and delivery.
5. **Avoid Over-Reaction to Student Discomfort:** While it's crucial to acknowledge and address student discomfort, avoid over-reacting by eliminating all potentially challenging elements. Instead, provide the necessary support and guidance to help students navigate these challenges, promoting a culture of empowerment and growth.

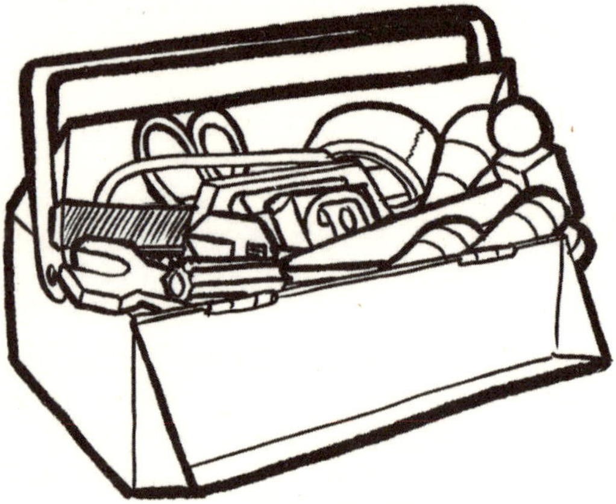

Ding's Toolbox: Threshold Concepts

Threshold concepts, fundamental and transformative ideas within a subject, serve as invaluable tools for learning designers. These concepts pinpoint core, challenging ideas that learners often find difficult. By integrating these concepts strategically, aligning them with assessments and activities, learning designers can enhance the overall teaching and learning experience.

1. **Selection:** Review the subject, identifying areas where learners typically struggle.
2. **Identify Potential Threshold Concepts:** Look for fundamental, transformative concepts with high educational value
3. **Integration:** Incorporate these concepts prominently in your learning design and introduce them at an appropriate point in the curriculum for maximum impact.
4. **Design Alignment:** Align assessments, activities, and resources to focus on these key concepts. Ensure learners engage with and master these concepts effectively.
5. **Adaptability:** Recognise that threshold concepts may vary among learners. Allow flexibility in teaching methods and resources to accommodate diverse learning styles.

Dear Ray,

I've been wrestling with a common issue among learners - procrastination. It's particularly evident when they hit those tricky threshold concepts. You know, those points where the subject matter gets really tough. How can learning design help mitigate this? Are there any strategies I can employ to ease them through these challenging spots?

Best, **Josh, San Francisco**

Dear Josh,

Ah, the battle against procrastination, and those threshold concepts, can be the trickiest terrain to navigate. Here are some tailored strategies to embed in your learning design:

- **Break through the surface tension:** Start with a task that's easy to achieve. It's like dipping your toes in before taking the plunge. This initial success can spur learners on.
- **Start in the middle:** Embrace non-linear thinking. Design modular assignments with independent tasks. Let learners choose the starting point that suits them best.
- **Find ways to make it more enjoyable:** Choice is key. Offer options that let learners pick or create projects that truly interest them. When they're invested, they're more likely to dive in..
- **Constrain time:** Time limits are surprisingly effective motivators. Short, focused tasks with clear time guidelines can challenge the perception of a never-ending assignment.

Wishing you success in your endeavours!
Warmest regards, Ray

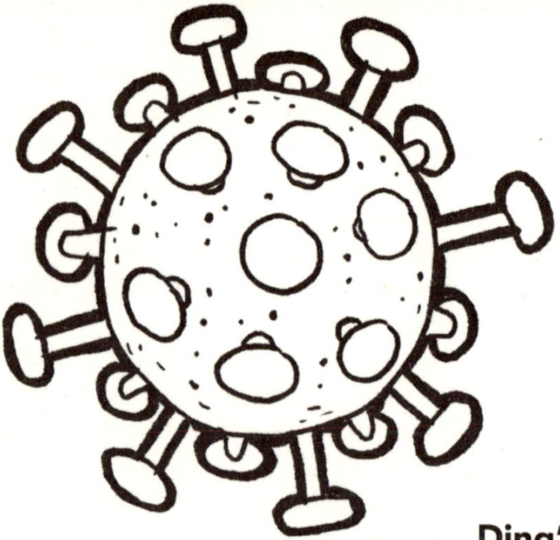

Ding's Covid Diaries:

Jumpers For Goalposts, Phil Gomm, May 2020 - Present

The COVID lockdowns brought about many unexpected changes, both positive and inspiring. People began to appreciate simple pleasures, like the beauty of bird songs and the inexplicable need to start baking pizza at the bottom of their gardens. It was a time when creativity flourished, much like those Labradoodles, popping up everywhere like Tribbles. For me, it was an opportunity to channel my energies into something engaging, a sort of creative holiday.

I realised that I wasn't alone in this desire. Many creative individuals, accustomed to working in artistic communities, were seeking a similar outlet. Amidst the online pop quizzes and kitchen discos, I saw a space for a creative challenge.

Numerous such challenges were already circulating, and while my idea wasn't entirely original, I conceived "The Kick-About." This concept drew inspiration from the sight of children playing football on imperfect, makeshift pitches. They used stones and jumpers for goalposts, demonstrating initiative and a focus on the game itself, not perfection. I liked the idea of a "kick about" allowing artists, creatives, and professionals to respond to creative prompts without the burden of tying it to their existing practice or professional work.

It was akin to creatives coming together for a spontaneous football match, purely for the joy of playing. The concept was straightforward: a prompt, shared on my blog, could be an artwork by a famous artist, a single word, or a photograph of an animal or phenomenon. Participants had to create new work in response to this prompt and submit it to me. I curated and showcased these submissions online, making them accessible to anyone who visited my blog.

To prevent the pressure of extended deadlines, I decided on a fortnightly schedule. The prompt was given on day zero, and the showcase happened on day 15, with the 14 days in between for creating new work. Drawing from my previous teaching experience, I knew that providing clear guidance and shorter timeframes could yield remarkable results.

This approach was inspired by a past project, an EU-funded initiative during my time as a course leader for an animation undergraduate program. Students visualized a piece of classical music over ten consecutive days. Each day, they created digital paintings in response to a section of the music. This project was a success, and it showed that shorter timeframes and precise guidance could lead to excellent outcomes.

The Kick-About's first iteration received a positive response, and it has now been running for over three years. This translates to a community of artists continuously producing new work under tight deadlines. The project has outgrown its initial pandemic-related context and has evolved into a platform for creative expression under specific conditions.

I also introduced this concept into my teaching endeavours. I've noticed that students are often accustomed to extended timelines for their projects, which can lead to procrastination. However, by challenging them to create work rapidly, I've witnessed remarkable breakthroughs and the enthusiasm that comes with producing new work under time constraints.

The folklore that good work requires prolonged struggles is something I challenge. I believe we can all relax more about creativity, embrace shorter timeframes, and see that impactful work can emerge from a quicker, more experimental process. My focus now includes examining the role of time in project expectations and how it influences learning and creativity.

Ultimately, what started as a distraction during the pandemic has transformed into a significant component of my thoughts on learning design and student behaviour. It has encouraged a re-evaluation of our fundamental assumptions about learning, creativity, and the time required to produce meaningful and transformative work.

Visit The Kick-About: philgomm.com/the-kickabout

"There's a lot that learning designers can learn from the success of the Kick-About. Firstly, it highlights how short 'sprints' with clear task guidance can move people to take action more quickly than distant deadlines. When we're designing learning, we should create activities that will help learners overcome procrastination and get started quickly.

Secondly, the Kick-About shines a light on the power of a community to drive engagement. When learners see other people producing work quickly, it can motivate them to overcome their own procrastination.

And thirdly, creating and sharing work 'in public' can be a powerful force for developing learners' creative confidence. The simple act of making work available on an open blog makes the activity much more real. As a result, learners care more."

The Sprint

A sprint is a time-bound, focused period for completing specific tasks. It encourages urgency, prevents open-ended work, and promotes rapid progress. Sprints drive productivity, accountability, and successful task completion.

Learning sprints offer focused intensity, preventing distractions and ensuring deep engagement. They enable rapid iteration through frequent feedback loops, enhancing effectiveness. Sprints are time-efficient, accommodating busy schedules, and are goal-driven, motivating learners with clear objectives. They also allow for easy adaptability to evolving learner needs or emerging trends.

"I've been incorporating sprints routinely into the design and delivery of my teaching for art and design students at a university in India.

One of the challenges I aimed to address is the connection between transmissive teaching and student procrastination. I wanted to encourage students to be more active immediately, disrupting the passivity of simply 'listening to their tutor on a Zoom call.'

By dividing the curriculum into sprints and encouraging a learn-by-doing approach, I've witnessed tangible and positive changes – and, personally, I've been having more fun too!"

Designing an Effective Learning Sprint

1. **Define the Sprint:** A learning sprint is a focused, time-bound period for acquiring specific knowledge or skills.
2. **Start with a Clear Vision:** Define your learning objectives, outcomes, and the specific skills or knowledge you want learners to gain.
3. **Set the Duration:** Determine the sprint's duration. Short, intense bursts work well, typically spanning a few days to a couple of weeks.
4. **Organise the Content:** Break the content into bite-sized modules or topics. Each should contribute to the overarching goal.
5. **Design Engaging Activities:** Develop activities, assessments, or exercises that challenge learners and align with the learning objectives.
6. **Incorporate Feedback Loops:** Integrate opportunities for feedback and reflection. Learners should regularly assess their progress.
7. **Schedule Milestones:** Set check-ins, deadlines, and milestones to keep learners on track. The rhythm is crucial for motivation.
8. **Foster Collaboration:** Encourage peer learning and support. Collaborative elements can enhance the sprint's effectiveness.
9. **Iterate and Adapt:** Continuously evaluate and adjust the sprint based on learner feedback and outcomes.
10. **Celebrate Achievements:** At the sprint's end, acknowledge and reward learners' achievements. Celebrate the completion of the learning journey.

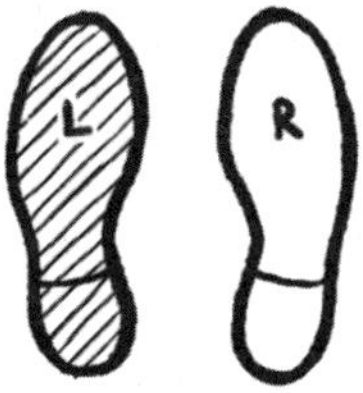

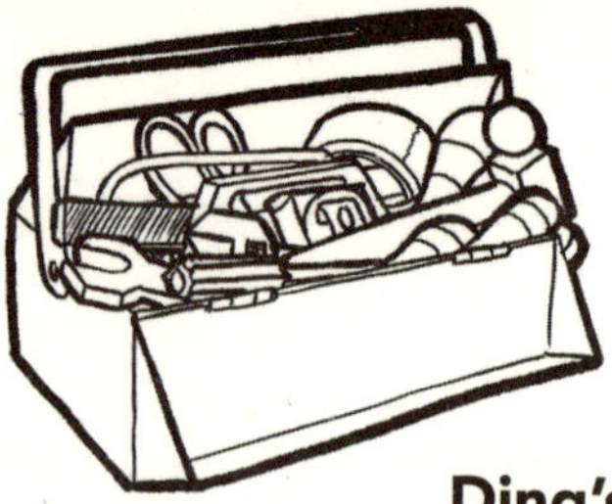

Ding's Toolbox: Discovery Learning

Discovery learning empowers learners to actively explore concepts, constructing knowledge through hands-on experiences and problem-solving. How to Use:

1. **Set the Stage:** Spark curiosity with a thought-provoking question, activity, or real-world problem.
2. **Encourage Exploration:** Allow freedom for investigation, providing guidance as needed.
3. **Foster Reflection:** Prompt learners to articulate findings and connect them to prior knowledge.
4. **Facilitate Discussion:** Engage in meaningful peer discussions to share insights and explore perspectives.
5. **Provide Guidance, Not Answers:** Offer prompts for problem-solving rather than immediate solutions.
6. **Assess Understanding:** Use formative assessments to gauge comprehension and identify areas for clarification.

Key Tips:

- Create an environment that encourages curiosity.
- Balance freedom with guidance for effective exploration.
- Encourage collaboration and peer learning.
- Emphasise discovery over rote memorisation.
- Provide real-world application opportunities.

Benefits:

- Promotes active engagement and motivation.
- Enhances critical thinking and problem-solving skills.
- Fosters deeper understanding and retention.
- Encourages ownership of learning.

Incorporating discovery learning empowers learners, fostering a deeper understanding of subjects. Provide support and resources for a successful experience.

Nicholas' Story

Education has been a part of who I am since I began teaching at twenty-one.

Reflecting on my journey, it's clear my passion for learning and education was ignited by my negative experiences as a student. While some people reminisce about a teacher who lit their educational path, I can't say I had a single one. Research carried out in the USA discovered that at the end of each academic year, most high school students liked a subject less than they had at the start. I can see why.

When I started studying at the UK's esteemed Slade School of Fine Art in 1970, I was hungry to learn. However, the first three weeks were spent waiting for classes to begin. Eventually I realised there were no classes; in fact, there was almost no teaching. The view was that education was for a talented elite who would grow on their own, given space and time. By being highly selective, the job was done before the students arrived.

While I was studying for my master's in Canada, I found that the institution prided itself on being 'tough'. I was part of a cohort of twelve students, and when only two of us graduated, the university deemed this to be a success because only those they considered to be the very best can have the qualification. To me, that was a dreadful failure. Rather than turning away from education, I used these experiences as a reference point and strove to model the opposite. For the first half of my teaching career, I did my best to show all those who had taught me how I would have liked to have been taught.

But after some years, I had a thought: why was I working so hard to convince people who had no idea what I was doing - and who in any case would probably soon be retired - or dead? To me, it was extremely important to be kind and supportive to those I taught, to let them be aware that I had confidence in their ability to succeed and to broaden their horizons.

In my career, I've taught in several countries and educational systems. These experiences have confirmed to me that poor teaching and learning design persists regardless of where you are (as does some very good teaching and learning design, although less often). When I first encountered a North American university, I thought, this is a learning paradise! It was like a learning supermarket with so much available, and at enrolment, you'd sign up for courses like taking goods off shelves. Highly-motivated students (and those who were resilient or 'tough') could then navigate this system.

But this approach to learning design largely left it to the student to fend for themselves, with a different group of peers for each course. A very large proportion of students would drop out. There could be many reasons for this, but there's no getting away from the fact that many students needed support, which they just weren't getting.

When I started teaching in North America, I discovered early career academics like me were given the largest first-year classes. These packed lecture theatres led many teachers there to adopt a performative style of teaching to keep the students entertained. I did likewise and enjoyed performing in that way and liberally sprinkling my lectures with jokes, which were greatly appreciated. My ego was boosted by the many students who told me how much they'd enjoyed my lectures. The trouble was, it was clear, when assessing, that little was being learned; they could often remember the jokes, but the content had been largely forgotten. This made me totally reassess my approach and led to a growing scepticism of the so-called 'inspirational teacher'.

Over the years, I sunk further and further into the background. I found that less is more, and that I could inspire much more effectively by not making the learning about me. As I write this, I feel uncomfortable with all the 'I's and 'me's. Yes, I very definitely try to model good practice. But this good practice means adopting a withdrawn role. My ideal class would be one where I would tiptoe out of the room, and nobody would notice, and the learning would continue as it had when I had been in the room. That approach is totally dependent on good quality learning design.

On returning to England, I took a position in an art school in the north of England. Not long after I started, an art teacher asked me, 'Why are you working so hard to prepare for your classes? I just stop at the greengrocer on the way to work and pick up something for the students to draw'. If that's the extent of the learning design, there will be precious little learning this point in my career, I was convinced that the real aim of teaching and learning design is to enable students to succeed. It sounds obvious, but too often people think when a student doesn't complete a course it's the student's fault. But I believe the opposite: the aim of learning design is to develop tasks that motivate students to learn and are challenging, but also achievable with the right support in place.

I'm grateful for all the educational experiences I've had; they have helped me see what's really important in teaching and learning design. Each anecdote, each classroom, has contributed to my understanding of what it means to be an effective educator. At the beginning of a course, students will be dependent on me. However, my aim is for them to reduce and finally cut this dependence. Nothing gives me greater pleasure as an educator than when students learn on their own and don't need me anymore.

Keep your eye out for Nicholas' postcards for more really useful insights from his travels in teaching and learning!

Ding's Hot Takeaways
from Nicholas's Story

1. **Individualised Support is Crucial:** Recognise the importance of providing individualised support to students. Acknowledge their unique needs and abilities and create a learning environment that empowers them to succeed.
2. **Balancing Challenge and Achievability:** Design tasks and assignments that strike a balance between being challenging and achievable. This helps to motivate students and fosters a sense of accomplishment when they complete tasks.
3. **Quality Over Quantity in Teaching:** Emphasise the quality of teaching over quantity. Rather than bombarding students with information, focus on creating meaningful learning experiences that promote deep understanding and retention.
4. **Shift from Performative Teaching to Effective Learning:** Move away from a performative style of teaching towards a student-centred approach. Encourage active participation and engagement and ensure learning is not solely dependent on the instructor's presence.
5. **Empower Independence in Learning:** Aim to gradually reduce students' dependence on the instructor. Create an environment where they feel confident in their ability to learn independently and celebrate their achievements when they demonstrate self-driven learning.

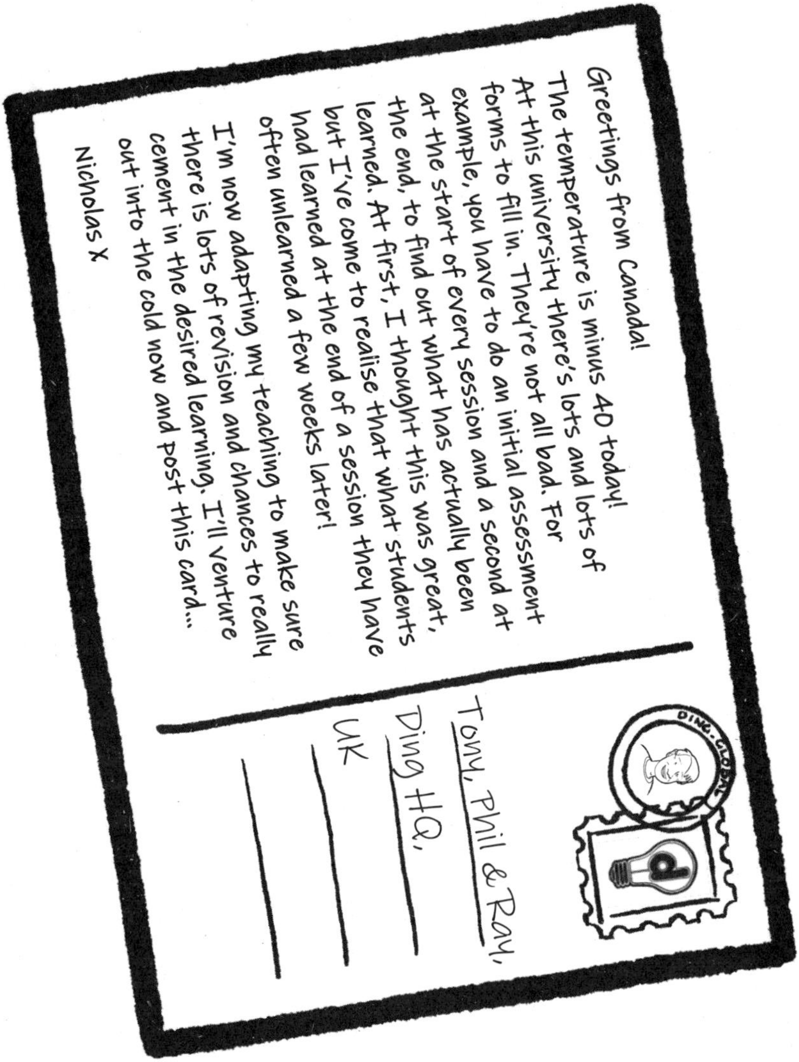
Greetings from Canada!
The temperature is minus 40 today!
At this university there's lots and lots of forms to fill in. They're not all bad. For example, you have to do an initial assessment at the start of every session and a second at the end, to find out what has actually been learned. At first, I thought this was great, but I've come to realise that what students had learned at the end of a session they have often unlearned a few weeks later!
I'm now adapting my teaching to make sure there is lots of revision and chances to really cement in the desired learning. I'll venture out into the cold now and post this card...
Nicholas X
Tony, Phil & Ray,
Ding HQ,
UK
DING.GLOBAL

Greetings from two kilometres in the sky!

This is my 1000th flight! All this flying means I've seen the security demonstrations so often I could recite the whole script. The cabin crew always look so bored when doing it and I've often thought that despite knowing the script, I'm unsure I'd actually be able to inflate a lifejacket...

It's difficult to think of any other way for airline passengers to learn about safety. All the same, this is a classic example of how ineffective passive learning is. Even when you know the script, you haven't learned what you need to.

This is an important lesson for when we're designing learning.

Nicholas X

Tony, Phil & Ray,

Ding HQ,

UK

given detailed instructions on what they should say and do, for every minute of the session. They were supposed to read the script which started with 'Good morning, my name is ... and I hope you're all ready to work hard today'.

As you'd expect, the trainers sounded wooden and weren't motivated and hence nor were their learners. It made me realise that, as learning designers, we provide an outline, which the teacher should then colour in. If they have no autonomy and no ownership of the material, then the session is doomed to fail.

As always, I'm learning the most from a bad example! Nicholas X

Tony, Phil & Ray

Ding HQ,

UK

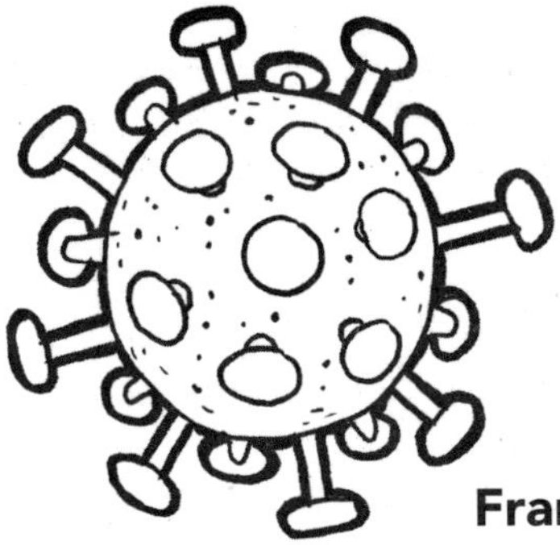

Ding's Covid Diaries:
Francesca Maxwell, July 2020
The benefits of teaching remotely

Francesca Maxwell is lecturer in Production Design for Animation at the National Film & Television School. In the very first episode of our podcast, ***The Ding-O-Meter***, we interviewed Francesca about her experience of moving online as a result of the COVID pandemic:

Ding: Can you share what you've enjoyed about teaching online in recent months, and what challenges you've faced due to the nature of your subject matter?

Francesca: *In a traditional setting, there can be a competitive atmosphere and a tendency to look over each other's shoulders. While this can be beneficial in some ways, it can also stifle individual expression. Teaching online offers more room for students to absorb information at their own pace and develop their own style.*

Ding: Have you noticed any students who might be struggling more with this shift, particularly those who thrive in a more extroverted, competitive environment?

Francesca: *Yes, indeed. Some students thrive in a more bustling, competitive setting. They feed off the energy and learn from each other's techniques. It's a dynamic that works for certain personalities. It's important to strike a balance and recognise that different individuals have different learning styles.*

Ding: Can you share some of the challenges you've encountered, particularly in terms of access to physical equipment for your subject matter?

Francesca: *Access to physical equipment is definitely a concern. For instance, when teaching painting techniques being present to observe and guide students is crucial. It's not just about showing them, but also ensuring they grasp the techniques effectively. Providing timely feedback is essential, and this can be more challenging in an online setting.*

Ding: Timeliness in feedback is crucial. How have you managed to address this aspect in an online environment?

Francesca: *Communication is key. I've emphasised the importance of staying in touch with students and finding effective ways to exchange information. Whether through photographs, video calls, or other means, it's about maintaining a constant line of communication. This ensures that I can be there for them when they're facing challenges.*

Ding: You've mentioned using various platforms. How have students responded to these diverse communication methods?

Francesca: *They've adapted well. By using different mediums, we've created a dynamic way of exchanging information. Students share their progress through images and updates, allowing for a continuous flow of communication. It's become an integral part of the learning process.*

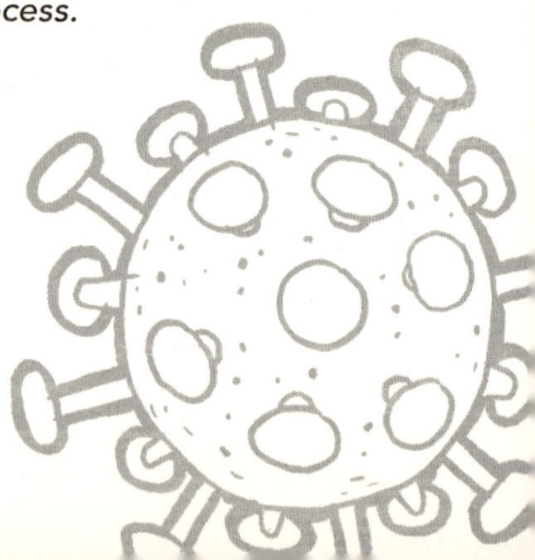

Ding: It seems like you've developed a system that suits the needs of both you and your students. Looking forward, what elements of online teaching do you plan to retain even when in-person classes resume?

Francesca: *The experiences of this period have shown us the value of remote learning. It's not about replacing traditional methods, but about integrating the best of both worlds. We've learned to be more independent and resourceful. I intend to continue incorporating these lessons into our teaching methods moving forward.*

Ding: Are there any aspects of your teaching style that you've reconsidered due to this shift to online teaching?

Francesca: *Certainly. I've reflected on the balance between providing information and allowing space for independent exploration. It's important not to overwhelm students with excessive content. Instead, I've learned to focus on what truly needs to be documented, while also encouraging them to ask questions and find solutions on their own.*

Ding: Finally, if you could offer one piece of advice to fellow educators navigating online teaching, what would it be?

Francesca: *I'd suggest not to see online teaching as a limitation. Treat it as you would any other teaching setting. Focus on the quality of interaction and the learning experience. The tool, whether it's digital or physical, is secondary. It's about connecting with students and helping them develop their skills and creativity.*

Ding's Hot Takeaways
from Francesca Maxwell's experience

1.Individual Expression: Online teaching allows for individual expression and self-paced learning.

2.Balancing Learning Styles: Recognise diverse learning styles and find a balance between competitive and independent approaches.

3.Challenges with Physical Subjects: Practical subjects like painting may face challenges in equipment access and hands-on guidance.

4.Avoiding Cognitive Overload: Focus on essential content to prevent cognitive overload and encourage independent problem-solving.

5.Timely Feedback: Use effective communication methods, including photos and video calls, for prompt feedback.

6.Diverse Communication: Use various platforms for dynamic information exchange and continuous learning

7.Value of Remote Learning: Integrate the best of both online and in-person methods for a resourceful learning environment.

The Ding-O-Meter

Welcome to **The Ding-O-Meter**, Ding's podcast, where we dive into engaging conversations with a diverse range of individuals sharing captivating insights, reflections, and experiences in the world of learning design and education.

From discussions on gamification and interface design to exploring the future of education, our podcast serves as a valuable listening and learning device.

Join us as we uncover the latest trends and thought-provoking ideas that shape the dynamic field of learning design.

ding.global/the-ding-o-meter-podcast

"Francesca's point about the importance of hands-on guidance in practical subjects like painting really hits home. It's not just about demonstration, it's about ensuring students truly grasp the techniques."

"Absolutely, Tony. It's a unique challenge in an online setting. One approach could be to create detailed, step-by-step video tutorials. This way, students can replay and pause as they practice."

"That's a good start. Additionally, we could incorporate virtual labs or simulation software for subjects like chemistry or engineering. It won't replace the real thing, but it offers a valuable supplement."

"Agreed. And considering Francesca's emphasis on constant communication, regular video check-ins could be beneficial. It provides a platform for students to ask questions and receive immediate feedback."

"You're right, Phil. And let's not forget about the potential of a 'flipped teaching' model. Assigning preparatory materials before a live session could make the virtual class time more interactive and focused on problem-solving."

"Absolutely. It engages students in a deeper way. Plus, it allows us to maximise the limited time we have in synchronous sessions."

"That's right, Phil, and by combining both online and in-person elements, we'll have even more tools at our disposal."

"True, Tony. This period has pushed us to explore new methods. The key is to keep refining and finding what works best for each subject."

"Indeed, it's about adapting and evolving. It's not enough to just deliver information, we have to design experiences that teach students how to learn."

Dear Ray,
I'm currently in the process of designing a course, and I'm concerned about overwhelming my learners with information. How can I ensure that the content is engaging without becoming too burdensome?
Mira, St Ives

Hello Mira,

Your concern is valid, especially in course design. It's crucial to consider cognitive load. Remember, our working memory has its limits, famously known as the "Magic No. 7" by George Miller. George Miller's Magic Number 7 refers to the cognitive psychology concept that the average person can hold about seven items in their working memory. Once we surpass this limit, retaining information becomes challenging

This insight has implications for designing effective learning experiences, suggesting that breaking information into manageable chunks can enhance comprehension and retention.

To address this further, start by activating your learners' prior knowledge. Encourage them to connect new material with what they already know. This provides a sturdy foundation for learning.

Additionally, engage both their visual and auditory senses simultaneously. When these channels work together, they create a more robust memory. Just ensure the content is coherent and meshes well.

Lastly, be selective. Focus on the key concepts rather than overwhelming them with every detail. Quality over quantity, as they say!

Best of luck with your designing.
Best wishes, Ray

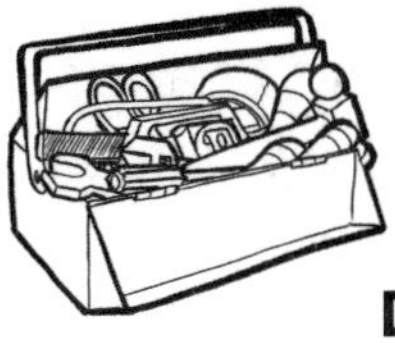

Ding's Toolbox: Cognitive Load Theory

Cognitive Load Theory posits that individuals have a limited capacity for processing information. **Intrinsic Load** refers to the inherent complexity of the learning material itself. Learning designers should align the intrinsic load with learners' expertise levels, gradually increasing complexity as they progress. **Extraneous Load** encompasses the additional cognitive effort required to process non-essential elements, such as confusing instructions or irrelevant information.

Cognitive Load Theory - A Brief User's Guide:

1. **Recognise Limits:** Acknowledge learners' finite information processing capacity. Design experiences within working memory constraints.
2. **Balance Intrinsic Load:** Assess inherent material complexity. Adjust challenge levels based on learner expertise.
3. **Minimise Extraneous Load:** Identify and eliminate unnecessary cognitive load. Streamline content for clarity and focus.
4. **Provide Clear Guidance:** Offer explicit, structured instructions. Guide learners without overwhelming them.
5. **Use Multimedia Wisely:** Integrate multimedia judiciously. Ensure visuals enhance understanding.
6. **Scaffold Learning:** Implement supportive scaffolding techniques. Break down complex concepts into manageable parts.
7. **Foster Active Engagement:** Encourage active learning and discussions. Deepen understanding to reduce passive reception.
8. **Evaluate and Iterate:** Continuously assess design effectiveness. Seek feedback and iterate for enhanced learning experiences.

Ding's Covid Diaries:
Spoiler Alert!, Phil Gomm, April 2021

At the climax of the original *Planet of The Apes* (1968), astronaut Charlton Heston makes an unsettling discovery.

In one of cinema's most celebrated twist endings, we discover, as he discovers, that the strange planet on which he crash-landed, is not some other alien planet to be escaped from, but the earth of the future. We know this, as Heston knows this, because we see the buried remains of the Statue of Liberty sticking out of the sand in the closing moments of the film. Turns out, our rugged hero has been living in the new normal all the time and didn't know it. Falling to his knees, Heston cries, 'I'm back. I'm home!'

I'm reminded of this sobering light-bulb moment when I think about those educators, who, having found their usual existence upended so completely by recent events dramatic and unexpected, are pinning their hopes on the restoration of what has gone before. Like our astronaut friend, they arrived with a nasty bump in this new world order and don't like it much. Unfortunately, I think they've got their own 'Statue of Liberty moment' coming their way.

Meanwhile, still on his knees before the ruins of an old ideal, Heston continues, 'We finally really did it. You maniacs! You blew it up!' Heston is referring to some earth-shattering apocalypse that undid all of mankind's achievements and set civilisation back apace. The pandemic has certainly felt a bit 'end of days' at times, with its emptied streets and grim statistics, and while it didn't blow everything to smithereens, it's certainly shaken most established practices in most established sectors to the core.

In response to the shaking-up of higher education specifically, there is a lot of chatter about institutions needing to make the switch to 'blended learning'. Put more starkly, in order to meet more of these uncertain times purposefully, HEI's must combine online and on-campus learning to transformative effect in order to survive. The post-coronial campus is hybrid, or it is extinct.

Hand on heart, I feel about this denouement the same way I felt about the ending of *Planet Of The Apes*, when I watched it for the first time as a kid, which is to say, I called it before the famous reveal. Sitting there in my *Spiderman* pyjamas, munching my way solemnly through a Wham Bar, I thought 'Duh, *of course* it's Earth'.

Was I a peculiarly precocious child, wise to the storytelling tricks of the trade I'd be teaching to undergraduates years later, in my role as course leader for an animation degree? Nope. The secret to my prescience was more mundane. *Planet of the Apes'* so-called alien landscape was already familiar to me from another movie with as outlandish a premise, *The Valley Of Gwangi* (1969), in which a bunch of cowboys find a living, breathing dinosaur stalking the crags and valleys of the Grand Canyon. Planet of the Apes wanted me to believe I was on some other world entirely, strange, unfamiliar, bizarre, only I didn't believe it for a minute. 'That's just the Grand Canyon', I thought to myself, fascinating terrain, sure, but not *alien*.

Which is why, I suppose, I'm a bit underwhelmed by the 'reveal' that blended learning is 'the future' for higher education. It is hard to feel a big 'wow' for a plot twist that comes as no surprise, or marvel at a paradigm shift that first presumes the landscape looks different, when, to my way of thinking, it looks the same as it ever did.

A concept can exist in practice before it is theorised, and so it was on the undergraduate programme my colleagues and I ran successfully between 2009 and 2019. As it happens, we were pioneering a horizon-scanning, pandemic-proofing exemplar of hybridity, only we didn't know it; or rather, we knew very well we were designing learning opportunities across a range of on-campus and online spaces, only we didn't have a name for it.

Okay, we did have a name for it; we called it 'problem-solving'. We mostly called it, 'How can we make stuff better?'

As it turns out, our 'house blend' was particularly rich, and, in terms of those 'all-important' student satisfaction scores, enjoyed by most.

In a pedagogical feat as ambitious as it was personally demanding, my colleague designed, produced, post-produced, and curated a 200+ curricula of pre-recorded instructional videos. The videos were hosted on a bespoke 'invite-only' website, giving our 100+ community of undergraduate students 24/7 access to the primary building blocks of their technical toolkit. This project wasn't initiated in response to some crisis, compelled into being by some institutional edict on e-learning, or posited as research. Simply put, it was the only way we could think of by which to make some of the course's unavoidably complex learning available to students, in a mode of delivery which itself could best mitigate that complexity. Instructional videos meant our students could 'chunk' their learning by pausing, rewinding, fast-forwarding and re-watching, and as many times as needed before the pennies dropped. My colleague had also dared imagine a new world for himself, wherein a large number of the life-sucking FAQs associated with the more rudimentary aspects of the course's technical curriculum, had been answered by him once and for all time.

I remember clearly the moment this same colleague figured out, with that great parcel of work in large part behind him, he could now use his student-facing time discursively. I remember because my colleague wasn't experiencing elation at his many accomplishments at the frontier of quality online learning, but a moment of acute existential angst. After all, having successfully produced a suite of precision-engineered instructional videos, had he not just ushered in his own obsolescence?

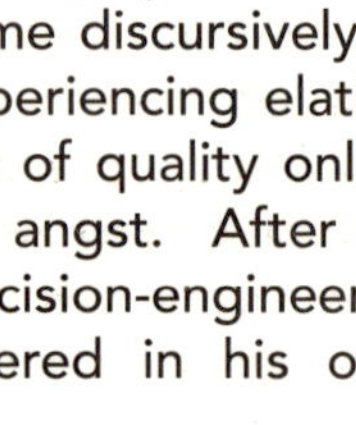

On the contrary, for not only had my colleague produced a rich resource of bespoke, asynchronous content, designed by him in the image of the sort of graduates our course was committed to producing, he'd also 'flipped his classroom'. I didn't use the word flipped, not back then, I just reminded him the thing students valued most about their proximity to experience and expertise was the opportunity to interact with the living, breathing human being who embodied it; that being talked 'at' by a well-designed instructional video was entirely useful, but interacting with tutors and their knowledge transformational.

As a result of all his hard work in producing online content for asynchronous delivery, my colleague was able to turn his on-campus classes into surgeries, lively and timely, responding to fresher debates deriving from learning already taking place in advance of his timetabled class. In addition to being the mouthpiece for his creative discipline, my colleague was now its think-piece too.

We also established a community of student blogs, a powerful online resource that went on to solve, mitigate, and transform a multitude of course management issues. In common with our curricula of instructional videos, we didn't introduce the blogging of student work as mandatory to get a jump on hybridity. Nor did blogs satisfy some pre-existing fascination of ours with online learning. We were looking for something by which to solve an immediate problem, in this instance, how to jump-start a more professionalised student culture of discursive creative development, by foregrounding formative feedback. We needed a way for students to make visible their creative development in a timely way: to us, to each other, to alumni, and to future employers. We wanted an interactive, iterative, and transparent tool, and blogging was our best and closest fit.

A few years on from this decision, and the hybridity between our online spaces and face-to-face interactions was truly a thing of grace, and the innovations kept coming. Long in advance of the emergency measures of COVID, we were paying sessional staff to engage remotely with our students, giving detailed formative feedback via the students' blogs. Our external examiner was able to review entire cohorts of student work, from week one to deadline day, without ever once leaving his office, in Edinburgh.

Even the University's VLE had its role to play in our special blend; one of my challenges, as the dedicated year one tutor, was to ensure students felt encouraged to try new things and work 'uncomforted' by their existing preferences. One way we did this was to ensure all students felt as 'new' as each other, by designing year one projects in which they were asked to develop work in response to conspicuously randomised prompts, meaning no one knew what to expect, and no one had any advantage. In service of this idea, I turned my on-campus briefings into 'events', with students picking slips of paper at random, the numbers on which related to pre-populated folders on the VLE. Once the students had picked their respective numbers, they went to their phones, logged into the VLE, and found their folders.

What was important about this bit of ritual was not me bringing students on to campus for a briefing, or the equally pedestrian fact of storing learning resources on a VLE, but rather the interplay between the characteristics of the two types of spaces: the communal one, in which everyone wanted to be there, at the same time, to experience something unrepeatable together, and the paperless accessibility of the university's virtual filing cabinet.

Meanwhile, all lectures, briefings and presentations were being recorded as audio files, and made available via the VLE, and likewise all our teaching materials, made available before those same lectures, briefings and presentations. None of this in the service of 'blending' you understand, but in the business of ensuring our students could reliably access what they needed, when they needed it.

If you're reading all this, thinking, 'Is there no end to this former course team's selfless commitment to their students?', while secretly grimacing at the goody-two-shoes-ness of it all, let me make an important admission: one of the biggest drivers for myself and my colleagues, in terms of a) building a brilliant resource of online tutorials, b) establishing a community of blogs and c) recording our lectures and flipping our classrooms, was to give ourselves the necessary confidence to stand firm in the face of querulous students: to be clear-eyed around our role and our responsibilities; to push back kindly, but keenly, and see off the worst excesses of the little emperor effect in some students brought about by the introduction of higher fees. So yes, our early embrace of hybridity was born out of a dream of all the ways we could enliven and enhance the student experience, but crucially, we undertook these projects to enhance our experience of managing students too.

And if all of this still grates, as maddeningly self-congratulatory, or smug, all I really mean to say is this: we made these changes, not as a response to the zeitgeist, to pressures external or otherwise, or in some bid for digital relevancy, but to bring about workable solutions in response to the goals we'd set for our community of learners, and for ourselves. We were not 'done unto' by technology, or somehow made subject to the abstractions of pedagogical best practice. These were our decisions, diversifying our delivery as and when it empowered us to do so.

Anyway, I get it.

Secretly, I feel it too.

There's just something under-powered about the term 'blended learning'. It is not an immediately exciting prospect. Somehow it reminds me of what happens to all those colourful straps of Plasticine I adored as a kid, and how, after a while, their former distinctiveness produced an unlovely, non-descript brown.

Given some of my less-than-highbrow references already cited here, it won't surprise you when I say that when I conceive of blended learning, I don't visualise some oatmeal smoothie, but Batman's utility belt circa 1966. When I think about blended learning, and when I talk about it with others, I'm imagining an array of discrete modes, techniques and tools, and all of them deployed in the delivery of awesome learning experiences - while seeing off as much of the mundanity of the educator's job role as humanly possible.

So, *duh* - obviously, blended learning is the future of higher education provision, but not because some global catastrophe has come along and made it so. Blended learning is what teaching looks like if you're building a student experience characterised by purposeful activities taking place in their most apposite environments.

And I'll tell you what blended learning *doesn't* mean, or rather shouldn't; it shouldn't mean the traditional on-campus lecture is somehow unwelcome, useless or dead. I have been electrified by keynote speakers and guest lecturers, who have turned their forty minutes or so of 'broadcast' into extraordinary delivery, made even more so because I was actually there. I challenge anyone who presumes to tell me I'm being rendered into passivity by an experience like that. Seems to me a traditional on-campus lecture would be an invaluable addition to your blend, but only if your lecturer is at their very best delivering in this most performative of spaces.

And blended learning doesn't mean cutting up your learning into small chunks and putting them online will make those activities magically better. If someone is cutting something up that is boring and putting it online, it is as ignorable there as anywhere else. Given the COVID-inspired zeal for reforming higher education, I fear there are already powerful individuals mistaking form for function, for whom 'blend the learning' will become an unthinking institutionalised goal in itself, which is the same as expecting the envelope to do the work of the letter. 'Students want blended learning'; agreed, and they'll get just that if the *design* of their learning is prioritised.

In the end, my experience, as an unwitting and rather unlikely champion of blended learning, comes down to this: it is the opportunity we've *always* had to be more imaginative, more creative and more precise in terms of learning design.

The prospect of blending your learning should feel as if you have the fullest array of tools at your disposal. These tools, these modes, these distinctive textures of teaching, need to be aligned absolutely with the effect you're seeking to produce in your learners, which begins with understanding that modes do have effects on learners, and that you are in the very special and specific business of facilitating those effects.

So, Mr Heston, go right ahead. You can rail at the sky. You can wish with all your might things were different, that there's some way back to the way things used to be. True enough, there *is* wreckage sticking out of the ground, not of civilisation as we know it, but of the monumental masonry of monomodal teaching; and yes, liberty is in ruins too, but only the liberty to go on designing education, and delivering it, poorly.

Ding's Hot Takeaways
from 'Spoiler Alert!'

1. **Adaptation and Hybridity:** Learning designers and educators must adapt to the evolving educational landscape. Blended learning, combining online and on-campus elements, is not a new concept but an adaptable approach to enhance the student experience.
2. **Purposeful Learning Design:** Learning designers should focus on purposeful and creative learning design, using a variety of tools and methods to align with specific learning outcomes.
3. **Precise Application:** Blended learning should not be approached as a one-size-fits-all solution but should be carefully tailored to achieve desired effects in learners.
4. **Avoiding Misconceptions:** Blended learning is not merely about putting traditional content online; it's about designing effective and engaging learning experiences.
5. **Championing Change:** Learning designers play a pivotal role in driving positive changes in education by using technology and creative pedagogy to enhance the student experience.
6. **The Role of Learning Design**: Learning design is a powerful tool that empowers educators to create meaningful and transformative learning experiences, bridging the gap between technology and pedagogy.
7. **Preparing for Challenges:** Learning designers must be ready to face challenges, manage student expectations, and continually adapt to meet the evolving needs of learners in the digital age.

Tony, Phil & Ray,
Ding HQ,
UK

Greetings!

This is the second year where I'm doing carousel timetable teaching. I've been told I have to give exactly the same lecture five times to different groups of students over the academic year. This is harder than it sounds, as I want to make changes and ad lib and do things differently.

Why oh why don't they simply record me doing the lecture and then free me up to do some proper teaching? When I suggested this, they weren't interested...

It's strange how university teaching is so reluctant to move out of the Middle Ages.

Nicholas x

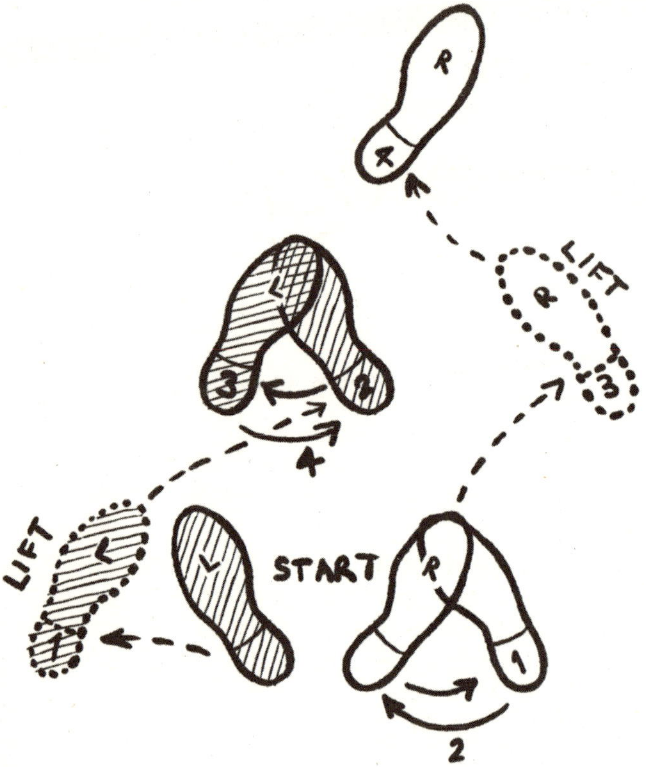

Doing The Flip

'Flipping' the classroom is a strategic move in learning design that reverses the traditional teaching approach.

Instead of introducing new concepts during class time, instructors provide learners with resources, like videos or readings, to explore beforehand. Classroom sessions are then dedicated to interactive discussions, problem-solving, and practical application of the pre-learned material.

Flipping the classroom is a classic learning design manoeuvre that shifts the focus from passive reception to active application. By pre-introducing content, valuable class time becomes a hub of interaction, ensuring a deeper grasp of the subject matter.

How to Flip

1. **Preparation Phase:** Select or create pre-learning materials that effectively introduce the topic. These can be videos, articles, or interactive modules.
2. **Distribution:** Provide learners with access to the pre-learning resources well in advance of the class. Ensure they have the necessary support to navigate and understand the content.
3. **Classroom Engagement**: During the class session, focus on activities that enhance understanding, such as discussions, group work, and hands-on exercises. Use this time for clarifications, debates, and practical application.

Benefits:

- **Enhances Active Learning:** Classroom time is maximised for engagement and application, promoting deeper understanding.
- **Individualised Pace:** Learners can absorb pre-learning material at their own speed, catering to diverse learning styles.
- **Effective Use of Resources:** Instructors can concentrate on guiding and supporting, rather than delivering content.

Considerations:

- **Access to Resources:** Ensure all learners have access to the pre-learning materials, addressing potential disparities.
- **Clear Communication:** Clearly communicate expectations and the rationale behind flipping the classroom for optimal learner buy-in.

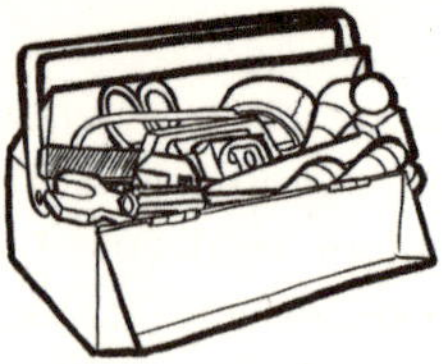

Ding's Toolbox: Constructivism

Constructivism, a key learning theory, asserts that learners actively build knowledge by connecting new information to their existing mental frameworks. For learning designers, leveraging constructivism enables us to create experiences that equip learners with higher order thinking skills. These skills are things like negotiating, debating, collaborating, directing, managing and co-creating, and they are arguably more important than subject knowledge.

Constructivism – A User's Guide:

1. **Activate Prior Knowledge:** Begin with learners' existing knowledge. Connect new information to prior experiences.
2. **Promote Collaboration:** Encourage group discussions and peer teaching. Build collective understanding through collaboration.
3. **Provide Authentic Tasks:** Design tasks reflecting real-world challenges. Enhance theoretical knowledge application.
4. **Facilitate Reflection:** Include reflective exercises for self-assessment. Use journaling and discussions for reflection.
5. **Offer Diverse Perspectives:** Present information from various viewpoints. Enrich learning with diverse perspectives.
6. **Create Active Learning Opportunities:** Implement hands-on activities and problem-solving. Deepen understanding through active engagement.
7. **Adapt to Learning Styles:** Recognise and accommodate diverse preferences. Provide flexible activities for different styles.
8. **Assess Understanding Continuously:** Use formative assessments for ongoing feedback. Adjust learning experiences based on continuous assessment.

Dear Ray,
I'm designing an online course and I'm a bit worried that my learners are going to feel isolated, working remotely from one another. What's your advice on how I can 'bake-in' a culture of collaboration?
Yours hopefully, **Geraldine, Glasgow**

Dear Geraldine,

Fear not, for fostering collaboration in an online course is indeed a common concern, but with the right learning design ingredients, you can create a culture of teamwork and peer engagement. Here's a few ideas for you to try:

- Create virtual breakout spaces for small group discussions, fostering teamwork.
- Design discussion forums with structured activities to prompt collaboration.
- Implement peer assessment for certain assignments, providing clear evaluation criteria.
- Incorporate group projects with assigned roles for each member.
- Host live sessions for Q&A and group discussions, enhancing real-time engagement.
- Use social learning platforms to encourage informal interactions and community building.
- Introduce gamification elements that reward teamwork and collaboration.
- Organise virtual 'coffee breaks' for casual conversations, fostering a social atmosphere.

By introducing these elements into your course design, you'll create a collaborative environment that transcends physical boundaries.

All the best, Ray

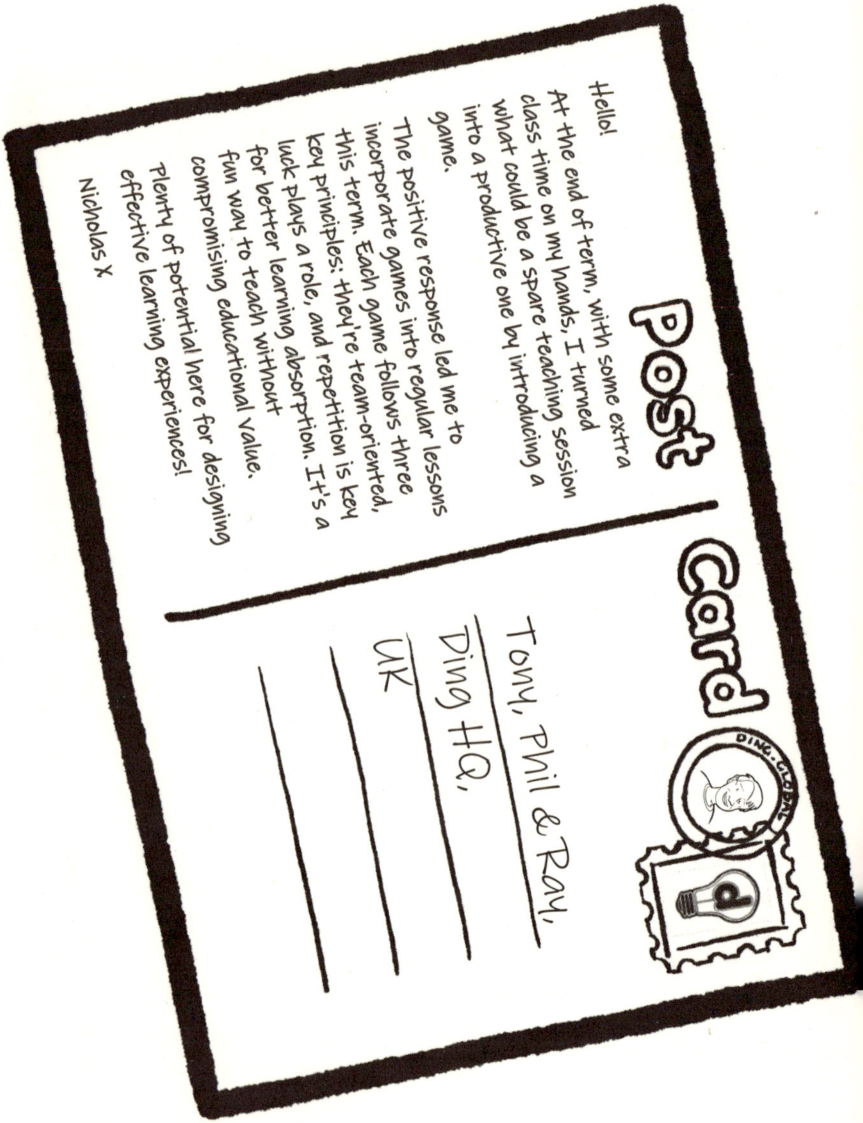
Post Card
Hello!
At the end of term, with some extra class time on my hands, I turned what could be a spare teaching session into a productive one by introducing a game.
The positive response led me to incorporate games into regular lessons this term. Each game follows three key principles: they're team-oriented, luck plays a role, and repetition is key for better learning absorption. It's a fun way to teach without compromising educational value.
Plenty of potential here for designing effective learning experiences!
Nicholas X
Tony, Phil & Ray,
Ding HQ,
UK
DING.GLOBAL

Card

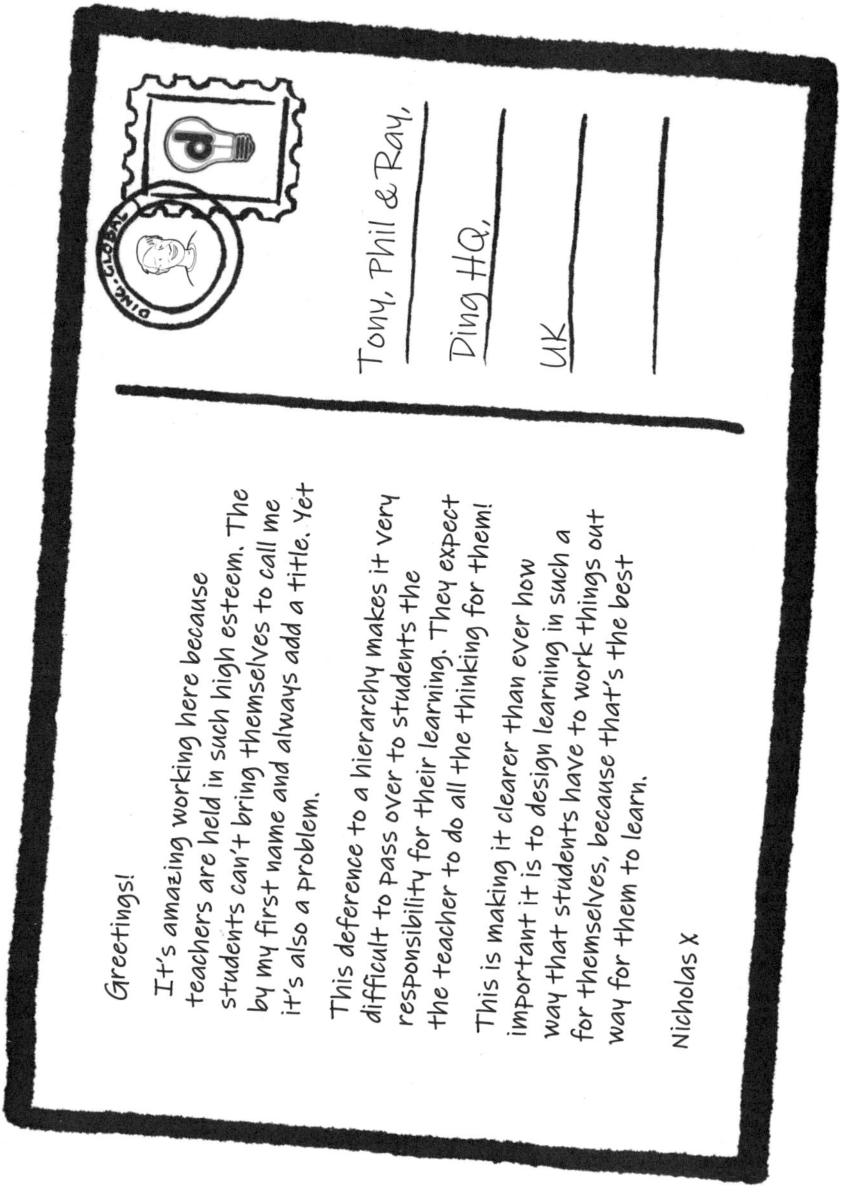
DINK-GLOBAL
Tony, Phil & Ray,
Ding HQ,
UK
Greetings!
It's amazing working here because teachers are held in such high esteem. The students can't bring themselves to call me by my first name and always add a title. Yet it's also a problem.
This deference to a hierarchy makes it very difficult to pass over to students the responsibility for their learning. They expect the teacher to do all the thinking for them!
This is making it clearer than ever how important it is to design learning in such a way that students have to work things out for themselves, because that's the best way for them to learn.
Nicholas X

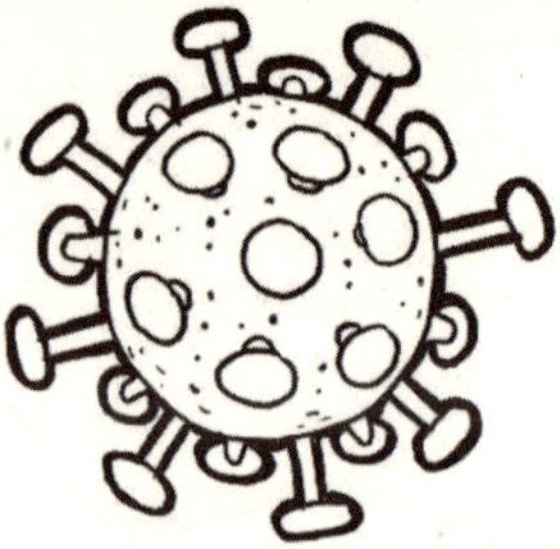

Ding's Covid Diaries:
Jeremy Hunsinger, April 2021

How to avoid the creepy treehouse of learning design

Back in September 2021 we spoke with Jeremy Hunsinger on the Ding-O-Meter podcast. Jeremy is Associate Professor of Communication Studies at Wilfrid Laurier University, Canada, and he introduced us to a series of post-pandemic metaphors well-suited to an episode of *Scooby-Do*: the 'professorial zombie,' 'data ghosts,' and 'creepy treehouses.'

Jeremy's metaphors illuminate the complexities and challenges of the post-pandemic learning environment and offer insights into mitigations for learning designers.

"The Professorial Zombie"

The term "professorial zombie" is a metaphorical concept used to describe a phenomenon in higher education, particularly in the context of online learning. It symbolises the idea that the traditional role of a professor may be reduced to a passive, automated entity in certain educational settings.

In this metaphor, the "zombie" represents a professor who, due to the increasing reliance on technological tools and platforms, may find their role reduced to that of a facilitator or a deliverer of pre-recorded lectures. They may lose some of the dynamic, interactive qualities traditionally associated with teaching.

The transformation into a "professorial zombie" can occur when technology takes over tasks that were once primarily performed by the instructor. For example, in some online learning environments, automated grading systems, chatbots, or pre-recorded lectures may handle certain aspects of instruction, leaving the professor with less direct involvement in the teaching process.

This concept highlights the potential risk of dehumanising the educational experience, as students may miss out on the personalised guidance, mentorship, and real-time interaction with their professors. It also underscores the importance of balancing technological advancements with the preservation of the essential human elements of teaching and learning

Educational institutions and learning designers should be mindful of this concept when implementing technology in education. While technology can enhance access and efficiency, it's crucial to maintain a balance that preserves the vital role of the instructor in fostering critical thinking, engagement, and meaningful learning experiences for students.

"The Data Ghost"

In the context of online education, the term "data ghosts" refers to the persistent digital traces left by students and educators in the virtual learning environment. These traces encompass various forms of data, including interactions, engagement metrics, assessment results, and other digital footprints generated during the online learning process.

For instance, when students participate in online discussions, submit assignments, take quizzes, or engage with learning materials in a digital learning management system, they leave behind a trail of data. This data may include timestamps, response patterns, navigation behaviours, and content preferences. Similarly, educators generate data through activities like designing course content, evaluating assignments, tracking student progress, and providing feedback.

These data ghosts continue to exist in the digital realm, even after the learning activity has concluded. They serve as a record of online learning interactions, providing insights into student performance, learning preferences, and engagement levels. Educational institutions and learning platforms often use this data to inform instructional design, personalise learning experiences, and assess the effectiveness of online courses.

However, it's crucial to consider the ethical and privacy implications associated with data ghosts in online education. Students and educators should be aware of how their data is collected, stored, and used by educational technology providers and institutions. Transparency and informed consent regarding data practices are essential for ensuring that individuals have control over their digital footprints.

Furthermore, institutions should implement robust data protection measures to safeguard sensitive information and comply with privacy regulations. Balancing the benefits of data-driven insights with the protection of privacy rights is a critical consideration in the design and implementation of online education platforms.

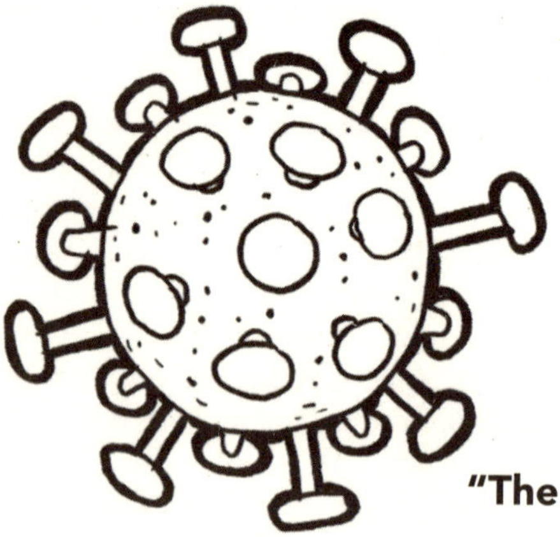

"The Creepy Treehouse"

The concept of the "creepy treehouse" in the context of education and digital learning refers to a situation where educators or institutions create online environments or platforms that, despite good intentions, come across as overly intrusive, contrived, or artificial to students. Much like a treehouse that a well-meaning adult might construct for children, the intention is to provide a space for learning and interaction. However, if the design feels forced or overly controlled, it can have the unintended effect of making students uncomfortable or feeling like their autonomy is being stifled.

The term "creepy" in this context does not imply any malicious intent, but rather highlights the unintended consequences of an overly prescriptive approach to online learning. It draws attention to the potential discomfort or unease that students may feel when presented with a learning environment that feels too contrived or imposing, possibly inhibiting their natural inclination to explore, discover, and engage with the material in their own way.

The key takeaway from the concept of the creepy treehouse is the importance of striking a balance between providing structure and guidance in online learning environments while also allowing for flexibility, creativity, and individual agency. This ensures that the learning experience remains authentic, engaging, and conducive to the diverse ways in which students learn and interact with educational content.

Ding's Hot Takeaways
from our conversation with Jeremy Hunsinger

1.Balancing Technology and Humanity: Learning designers need to ensure that technology enhances, rather than replaces, the human element of education. Strategies like real-time interactions and open communication are crucial to prevent the 'zombie' effect.

2.Prioritising Data Privacy: Institutions and designers must establish clear policies on data collection and usage. Students should have control over their own data, and education about digital privacy should be provided.

3.Empowering Learner Agency: Avoid creating 'creepy treehouses' by involving students in the design and decision-making processes. This fosters a sense of ownership and active participation in their learning journey.

4.Recognising Unintended Consequences: The shift to online learning brought unintended consequences. Acknowledging these challenges is essential for creating a more holistic and engaging online learning experience.

5.Preserving Human Interaction: While technology is a powerful tool, it should not overshadow the vital role of the instructor in facilitating engagement, critical thinking, and meaningful learning experiences.

6.Ethical Use of Data: As data ghosts persist, ethical considerations become paramount. Transparency and informed consent regarding data practices are essential to protect privacy rights and ensure individuals have control over their digital footprints.

The Desire Path

Imagine a park with neatly paved pathways, but despite the planning, people consistently forge their own shortcuts across the grass. These are desire paths, representing the most direct route between where one stands and where one wants to go.

In urban planning, some have opted to delay paving pathways until desire paths naturally emerge. This allows planners to construct routes that align with people's actual journeys.

For learning designers, recognising these desire paths can be a game-changer. Before embarking on a learning activity or program, investigate the technologies your learners already gravitate towards and ponder why. Consider if these technologies are suitable for your purposes. Even if they aren't, understanding the appeal of a particular technology offers valuable insights.

One prevalent issue in online learning design is the belief in a "build it and they will come" philosophy. There's a surplus of platforms and apps available for supporting learning. Focusing on the ones your learners already use can be the key to unlocking their engagement.

However, you might find yourself in a situation where you need to use a specific technology or platform, like a Virtual Learning Environment (VLE) or Learning Management System (LMS). If this isn't your learners' preferred choice, be prepared to invest effort in familiarising them with it. Consider how you can leverage their existing habits to guide them to the desired learning destination.

By identifying and understanding these desire paths, learning designers can create more effective learning experiences. This involves aligning technological choices with learners' preferences, ultimately leading to higher engagement and more impactful learning outcomes.

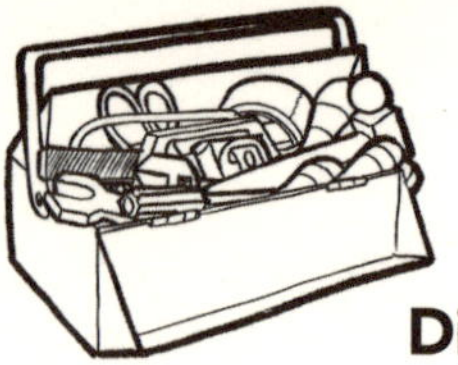

Ding's Toolbox: Behaviourism

Behaviourism underlines the profound influence of the learning environment on human behaviour. As learning designers, we can strategically use this insight to craft dynamic learning experiences. Let's explore key applications:

1. **Environmental Influence:** Thoughtful design of physical and digital spaces can significantly impact the learning experience, considering layout, lighting, and ambiance.
2. **Positive Reinforcement:** Acknowledging and rewarding desired behaviours through digital platforms encourages active engagement and sustains learner participation.
3. **Inclusivity and Diversity:** Creating inclusive environments anticipates diverse learner needs, ensuring all feel comfortable and empowered to engage with the material.
4. **Learner Empowerment:** Allowing learners to shape their learning environment fosters a sense of ownership and autonomy, leading to increased engagement.

Tips:

- Pay attention to the look and feel of both physical and online learning spaces.
- Use things like emojis, comments and 'likes' to show learners you have seen their contributions.
- Anticipate you will have someone who is deaf, someone blind, a non-native speaker, a dyslexic, a dyspraxic and an autistic learner when you are designing an experience.
- Actively involve learners in personalising their learning environment, both physical and online where possible.

Benefits:

- Boosted learner engagement and participation.
- Enhanced motivation and a positive learning experience.
- Improved inclusivity, catering to diverse learner needs.
- Heightened ownership and investment in the learning experience.

Dear Ray,

I've been pondering over ways to alleviate the anxieties that learners often experience when they embark on a new course. Transitioning to university can be quite overwhelming for them, and I want to make it as smooth and welcoming as possible. What advice can you offer to help me design a more supportive experience for these fresh-faced learners? Any tips on prioritising their social integration and wellbeing?

Ashish, London

Dear Ashish,

Firstly, kudos to you for recognising the importance of easing those initial jitters for our incoming learners! Here are some nuggets of advice:

- **Enhance Student Wellbeing:** Design interactive activities to foster connections, address isolation concerns, and promote inclusivity.
- **Foster Positive Mindsets:** Incorporate reflective exercises, introducing concepts like Carol Dweck's growth mindset. Carol Dweck's growth mindset concept emphasises the belief that individuals can develop their abilities and intelligence through dedication, hard work, and learning from setbacks. It contrasts with a fixed mindset, which assumes that abilities are innate and unchangeable.
- **Prioritise Small Groups:** Opt for small group inductions to encourage team building and socialisation.
- **Ensure Accessible Support:** Make support resources easily accessible for students, guiding them on seeking help.
- **Detail Matters:** Pay close attention to administrative aspects; small details can have a significant impact.
- **Avoid Assumptions:** Never assume students' knowledge; provide clear and concise guidance when needed.

Wishing you all the best in creating an engaging and anxiety-free onboarding experience for your learners!

Warm regards,
Ray

"Hey Tony, back when I was course leader, I gave my time, energy and resources to creating a really welcoming baseroom for my students. I painted the walls nice colours, hung posters on the walls, designed the lighting. Some of my academic colleagues didn't get it. They said, 'You're an educator, not a painter and decorator...'"

"Little did they know you weren't so much 'painting and decorating' as 'learning designing'. You just didn't know it yet, Phil!"

"I've never thought about it that way before, but you might be right, Tony. The link between my students' engagement with their course and their engagement with their learning environment just seemed obvious to me. I wonder how many other people are thinking in just these joined-up ways about creating effective learning experiences, but who wouldn't identify as learning designers?"

"I think you're onto something, Phil. Learning design is an intersectional skillset, combining expertise in education, technology, psychology, user experience, content development, inclusivity, data analysis, project management, adaptability, and communication.

It brings together a bunch of skills and knowledge from different areas. It's not just about creating courses; it's also about understanding how people learn, using tech effectively, making content engaging, and ensuring everyone can access it. So, in a way, learning designers are the problem-solvers of the learning world, bringing a bit of everything to the table."

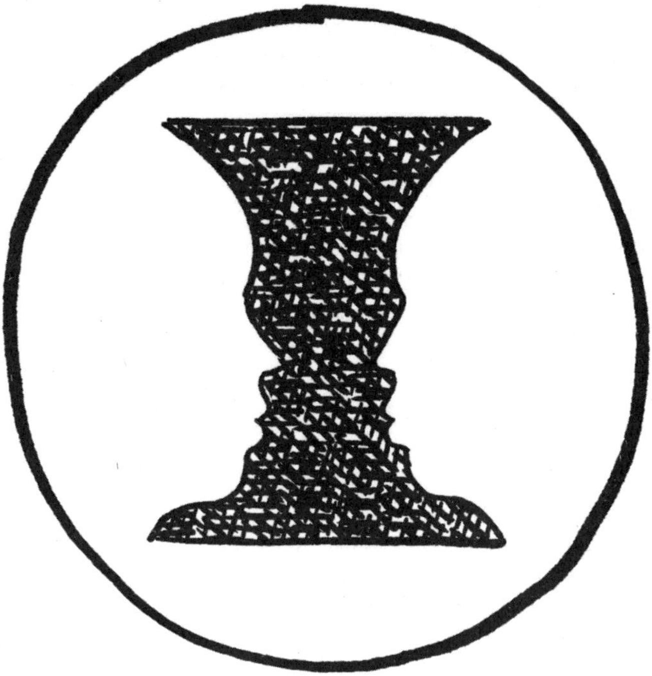

Are You A Hidden Learning Designer?

Rubin's Vase is an optical illusion that illustrates how our perception can shift between two distinct images.

In much the same way, the role of a learning designer often remains at the periphery of a more conspicuous skillset, much like the "vase" in the illusion. Yet, this "invisible" learning designer is, in fact, the force behind the scenes, forming the very skills and knowledge that constitute the more conspicuous aspect of education.

Learning design is about creating the ideal conditions for individuals to engage with new information, comprehend complex concepts, and acquire valuable skills. Learning designers are the unsung heroes of education, shaping the way knowledge is imparted and absorbed.

In today's rapidly evolving educational landscape, where traditional methods are being augmented or replaced by digital and remote learning, the role of learning design has surged in importance. The demand for this skillset is more pressing than ever, and for good reason:

1. **Adapting to a Shifting Landscape:** Recent global events have accelerated the transition towards online and blended learning. Learning designers stand at the forefront of this shift, ensuring that learning experiences remain effective and engaging.
2. **Elevating the Student Experience:** Education is no longer just about knowledge transfer; it's about providing a meaningful and transformative experience for learners. Learning designers are instrumental in using technology and innovative pedagogy to bridge the gap between traditional teaching and the digital age.
3. **Personalising the Learning Journey:** AI has significantly improved the ability to personalise learning. Learning designers are now able to create truly personalised learning paths that cater to individual needs
4. **Harmonising Technology and Teaching:** More than ever, there is a need to ensure technology is working to support, not obstruct, learning. Learning designers are adept at leveraging theories, tools and platforms to create seamless learning experiences.
5. **Assessing and Refining Impact:** Learning design is more than just content creation. Learning designers can help businesses set clear objectives, then design experiences to ensure learners and employees have the knowledge and skills to achieve the objectives.

Here are some job roles that often involve learning design skills, even if it's not explicitly mentioned in the title:

1. **Instructional Designer:** Instructional designers are explicitly focused on creating effective learning experiences.
2. **Curriculum Developer:** They design and develop educational materials and resources, which inherently involves learning design principles.
3. **E-learning Developer:** This role involves creating online educational content, which requires a strong understanding of learning design.
4. **Educational Technologist:** They work with educators to integrate technology into teaching, requiring knowledge of effective learning design.
5. **Training Specialist:** Often involved in creating and delivering training programs, which involves designing effective learning experiences.
6. **Content Developer:** In educational settings, content developers are often responsible for creating engaging and effective learning materials.
7. **Educational Consultant:** Consultants often work with institutions to improve teaching and learning practices, which involves learning design.
8. **Learning Experience Designer:** While similar to instructional design, this role often involves a broader approach to designing holistic learning experiences.
9. **Academic Advisor:** While their primary role is advising students, they often contribute to the design of support materials and resources.
10. **Subject Matter Expert (SME):** SMEs often incorporate learning design principles to enhance how they share their expertise.
11. **Librarian:** They often play a role in curating and recommending educational resources, which requires an understanding of effective learning design.
12. **Online Community Manager:** In online education settings, this role often involves facilitating discussions and interactions, a key aspect of learning design.

Quiz: Are You A Hidden Learning Designer?

1. When approaching a learning task, what interests you most?

a. Designing how the content is delivered
b. The subject matter itself
c. Facilitating discussions and interactions
d. Ensuring accessibility and inclusivity

2. How would you describe your approach to problem-solving in an educational context?

a. Considering various instructional strategies
b. Focusing on content delivery and understanding
c. Encouraging collaboration and peer learning
d. Ensuring diverse learning needs are met

3. What aspect of teaching do you find most rewarding?

a. Creating engaging learning experiences
b. Sharing knowledge and expertise
c. Fostering a supportive and interactive learning environment
d. Promoting equity and accessibility in education

4. How do you feel about integrating technology into the learning process?

a. Excited, and I'm always exploring new ed-tech tools
b. Comfortable, but I prefer traditional teaching methods
c. Enthusiastic, especially for enhancing student interactions
d. Committed to ensuring technology is inclusive and accessible.

5. In a learning environment, what do you consider your primary role?

a. Designing effective learning experiences
b. Delivering content and explaining concepts
c. Facilitating discussions and group activities
d. Ensuring all learners can access and benefit from the content

6. What do you believe is the most crucial aspect of a successful learning experience?

a. Engaging instructional design
b. Clear and comprehensible content
c. Active participation and collaboration
d. Inclusivity and accessibility for all learners

7. How do you approach the challenge of diverse learning styles in a class?

a. Designing adaptable instructional strategies
b. Providing various resources for content understanding
c. Encouraging peer support and collaborative learning
d. Ensuring materials are accessible to all learners

8. What aspect of education do you believe has the most significant impact on learners?

a. Well-designed learning experiences
b. Quality content and effective delivery
c. Interactive and engaging learning environments
d. Inclusive practices and accessibility

"To find out your scores, turn to the next page!"

Quiz: Are You A Hidden Learning Designer? Your Scores

If you answered mostly A's, then you likely possess the mindset and skills of a hidden learning designer. Your focus on designing effective learning experiences demonstrates your affinity for learning design.

If you answered mostly B's, you have a strong emphasis on content delivery and understanding, which is a valuable aspect of teaching. Consider exploring learning design principles to enhance your instructional strategies.

If you answered mostly C's, your emphasis on interaction and collaboration indicates a natural inclination towards facilitating engaging learning environments. Incorporating learning design principles can further amplify these strengths.

If you answered mostly D's, your commitment to inclusivity and accessibility showcases a crucial aspect of learning design. Consider exploring how you can integrate more instructional design elements into your approach.

"Remember, being a learning designer means you have a lot of power to shape and influence how people learn. Strengthening your knowledge of learning design principles, theories and techniques will further increase your ability to help your learners experience success."

Ding's Learning Design Bootcamp

Maybe it's time you activated your inner learning designer? Maybe you want to understand more about the role? Or maybe you're already working as a learning designer and you want to enhance your skills and connect with like-minded people?

Ding's Learning Design Bootcamp is for learning specialists, teachers and trainers who want to create better learning experiences. Our guided activities, jargon-free explanations and personalised feedback help you design learning that produce real impact. This is how it works:

- **One 60-minute live session, 7 videos and 3 activities per week**

The Ding team will guide you through activities that enable you to apply what you're learning. And they're fun too!

- **Slack-based community and 1-2-1 support**

Slack is our classroom and provides easy, flexible access to the Ding team. We also support you with 1-2-1 coaching sessions to discuss your specific questions and requirements.

- **Personalised feedback on your assignments**

Feedback is the thing that drives effective learning. You'll receive personalised feedback on all your module assignments to help you develop your learning design knowledge and skills.

You'll learn about 6 core principles of effective learning design: **Empathy, Curriculum, Inclusivity, Technology, Facilitation and Community**. Each principle is supported by extensive research into the factors that produce effective learning experiences.

Our Learning Design Bootcamp gives you the mindset and skillset to become an exceptional Learning Designer! For more information on **Ding's Learning Design Bootcamp** visit:

- **ding.global/learning-design-bootcamp**

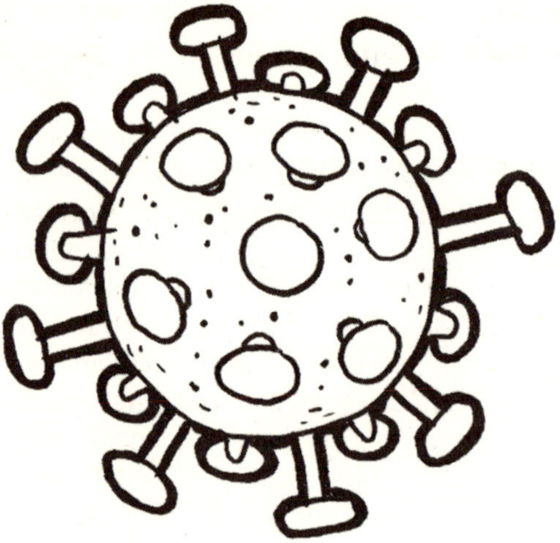

Ding's Covid Diaries: On Disruptions, Tony Reeves, December 2023

Goodness, we've reached the end already! Over the course of this book, we've explored the learning design lessons learned through and beyond the Covid pandemic.

We've also traced the origins of Ding in this tumultuous period in humanity's history, and I would like to say a huge thank you to everyone who has so kindly shared their experiences. Your insights have helped the Ding team appreciate the power of learning design to change lives. You have also helped us refine our views about what learning design is and can be and have inspired us to keep supporting and contributing to the learning design community.

But just as we thought things were returning to a place of relative stability, a new player has emerged: Artificial Intelligence. Fresh from the disruption of the pandemic, AI has brought a new wave of soul-searching for learning designers and educators everywhere. Will learning design be automated out of existence? Will humanity be taken over by robots? And will the essay be forever consigned to the dustbin?

Yet, just like Covid, AI has proved to be an accelerator. AI-enabled technologies make it possible for us to generate content at a pace that once seemed impossible. But just as with many technological inventions, speed does not always equal quality. AI simply accelerates our capacity to move – if we were moving in the wrong direction to begin with, AI will take us even further off course.

And similar to the feeling of hope produced by the end of the pandemic, I find myself once again experiencing a sense of hope. As I write this, I'm currently guiding a new cohort of participants through Ding's Learning Design Bootcamp. AI is making it possible for these budding learning designers to apply learning theories more confidently, iterate session plans more quickly, and develop learner personas more comprehensively.

When learning designers combine AI with well-researched theories of effective learning, they can produce ideas for engaging learning experiences more effectively, and more rapidly. Now there are no excuses for poor teaching and learning design: the tools exist to make effective learning experiences available to everyone.

The same goes for assessment – AI shifts the focus away from writing essays, answering multiple choice questions and sitting exams towards assessing learners' ability to question, iterate and evaluate. AI also does away with the problem of essay mills and plagiarism: instead, it places the onus on us as learning designers to design assessments that assess higher-order thinking and problem-solving skills, instead of testing students' ability to memorise information.

And let's not forget the creative potential that AI unlocks. It invites us to think expansively and iterate rapidly. It helps us become less precious about the first thing we create, and to focus instead on tailoring each learning experience to meet the needs of the intended learners. It helps us move away from the factory model of education developed during the industrial revolution and towards a more personalised learning experience. The technology is now available, it's up to us as learning designers to harness it effectively.

I know AI is not a panacea, and as with all technologies it must be treated with care and caution. When Phil and I first set up Ding, we discussed the idea that learning design is about pragmatism. Learning design enables us to cut through bias and personal preferences in teaching and learning, and instead focus on the most appropriate design for a specific experience. Despite the concerns and caveats surrounding AI, I believe it accelerates pragmatism in learning design. It enables learning designers to develop, test, iterate and refine learning experiences in order to deliver the optimal conditions for an individual or a group of learners. And it forces us to challenge outdated approaches to teaching, learning and assessment.

More than ever, businesses, schools and universities need to provide learning experiences that really move the needle. As humanity grapples with the biggest challenges it has ever faced, we as a species need to ensure all generations develop the knowledge and skills required to survive and thrive in the 21st century.

As we move beyond the pandemic and on into an uncertain future, a healthy dose of pragmatism in learning design feels like a jolly good thing to me.

Got more questions about Learning Design?
Want to book a strategy session with Tony & Phil?
How about a sprint to design a new learning product?

Drop us a line at **hello@ding.global**
or visit **ding.global**

We'd love to hear from you!

ding